Write Grants, Get Money

Second Edition

Cynthia Anderson
and Kathi Knop

Linworth
Books

Professional Development Resources for
K-12 Library Media and Technology Specialists

Library of Congress Cataloging-in-Publication Data

Anderson, Cynthia, 1945-
  Write grants, get money / Cynthia Anderson and Kathi Knop. -- 2nd ed.
    p. cm.
  Includes bibliographical references and index.
  ISBN-13: 978-1-58683-303-9 (pbk.)
  ISBN-10: 1-58683-303-0 (pbk.)
  1. Library fund raising--United States. 2. Proposal writing in library science--
United States. 3. Proposal writing for grants--United States. 4. School library
finance--United States. 5. Instructional materials centers--United States--
Finance. I. Knop, Kathi. II. Title.
  Z683.2.U6A53 2008
  025.1'1--dc22

                              2008022038

Carol Simpson: Editorial Director
Judi Repman: Consulting Editor

Published by Linworth Publishing, Inc.
3650 Olentangy River Road
Suite 250
Columbus, Ohio 43214

Copyright © 2009 by Linworth Publishing, Inc.

ISBN 13: 978-158683-303-9
ISBN 10: 1-58683-303-0

5 4 3 2 1

Table of Contents

Table of Contents *continued*

Table of Contents *continued*

Table of Contents *continued*

Table of Contents *continued*

Table of Contents *continued*

Table of Contents *continued*

Table of Figures

Table of Contents of
Write Grants, Get Money, 2nd Edition CD

Write Grants, Get Money, 2nd Edition, offers many bonus features, including a CD. On the CD are copies of funded grants, examples of curricula vitae and resumes, and a PowerPoint presentation on grant writing written by Dr. Gail Dickinson.

E. Judi Repman: Vita - long version

F. Judi Repman: Vita - short version

III. Sample Education Foundation Library Promotion

These resources are included to give the reader a sense of what types of support and grant programs can be offered when a foundation is organized to support a school district.

  A. SMEF Cover to Cover Brochure

  A brochure is included that describes a long-term foundation fund-raising program to fund K-12 school libraries with books and materials to update an old and limited budget collection.

  B. SMEF Cover to Cover Letter of Intent

  This letter of intent is an example of what could be sent to participants who wish to contribute to a school district foundation drive for a large library fund raiser.

  C. E2 Grant program 2006-2007

  An example of a grant opportunity sponsored by a foundation designed to support a K-12 school district is offered. This is a major, long-term fund raising program that could be used as a model to develop a similar plan to raise funds for school libraries.

  D. E2 Grant Recipients 2007-2008

  These examples of actual grants funded by a foundation designed to support a K-12 school district can give the reader an idea of the types of grants that might be funded for other libraries and classrooms.

IV. PowerPoint for Grant Seekers by Dr. Gail Dickinson

Included on the CD is an actual multimedia presentation that may be used to teach people how to write grants. It was written by Dr. Gail Dickinson, assistant professor at Old Dominion University.

Acknowledgments

Many thanks go to all the generous educators and librarians who shared their time and talent to provide us with real examples of grants, presentations, resumes, and curricula vitae. You are an amazing group of professionals. Special thanks go to Brooke Anderson for the drawings, to Terry Wintering for the awesome help and expertise, and to Rebecca Morrison, director of the Shawnee Mission Education Foundation, for sharing the campaign materials for their amazing fundraising drive for school libraries. Many thanks to Debi Affentranger, Janet Affentranger, Shonda Brisco, Barbara Brownlee, Patricia Conover, Chris Gustafson, Ann Harrity, Ronda Hassig, Suzanne Jensen, Mary Pat Meharry, Susie Nightingale, Jane Doe, Gail Dickinson, and Judi Repman for sharing so generously.

About the Authors

Cynthia Anderson is associate superintendent emeritus of a large suburban school district. She has served as a school librarian, school principal, and district director of libraries. She is a Milken Family Educator and has published articles in several journals. Her other Linworth books are *Write Grants, Get Money (1st Edition)* and *District Library Administration: The Big Picture Approach*.

Kathi Knop is a middle school library media specialist in Shawnee Mission, Kansas. She has been a librarian for nine years and has served as an elementary, high school, and middle school librarian. Kathi was an elementary school teacher for 10 years before getting her MLS.

Kathi graduated from William Jewell College in Liberty, Missouri, with an A.B. in elementary education and received a Masters of Library Science from Emporia State University.

Introduction

With just a little help from resources and contacts, any school library media specialist can write a winning grant proposal. *Write Grants, Get Money, 2nd Edition* was written to provide just such assistance to school library media specialists. This volume offers help to those who want to write grants in order to provide technology and other necessary and creative materials and services for their library media centers.

After writing or collaborating on many winning grants and sharing grant-writing strategies at conferences and seminars, we wanted to share those strategies in a book for school librarians. The purpose of *Write Grants, Get Money, 2nd Edition* is simple: to help school librarians get grant money for their schools. All school librarians and educators who want more for their libraries, schools, and classrooms than their budgets allow should have a copy of *Write Grants, Get Money, 2nd Edition*. This K-12 resource was written exclusively for school media specialists, their administrators, and colleagues who need tips on finding funding and collaborating with others to write grant proposals, so they can enhance their school library programs and facilities and make a difference for students. This easy-to-read, to-the-point guide is a practical tool targeted specifically at the overworked, underfunded school librarian. The authors are practitioners who have tailored a wealth of information to help busy school media specialists acquire the technology, materials, and services they need to achieve their dreams.

Grant writing can seem daunting and mysterious. For some people, the hardest part of writing a grant proposal is cracking the ice and putting their toes in the chilly waters of grant proposal writing. Once they make that first attempt and write a proposal, each subsequent effort seems a little easier. Their confidence grows.

For others, getting larger and more complex grant funding seems out of reach. They have landed some $250 to $500 grants, but cannot seem to break through to the big dollar grants. No matter where the reader is on the grant-writing continuum, she will find the information in this book practical and useful.

Content

Write Grants, Get Money, 2nd Edition is a valuable asset to the school library media specialist who wants to provide more for the students in his school because it will ease him into the field of writing grants. The book includes up-to-date resources, writing and editing tips, resource lists, sample grants, sample resumes and curricula vitae, as well as the encouragement librarians need to start or continue writing winning grant requests.

Arrangement

The book is conveniently arranged in chapters covering the topics about which most potential grant writers need more information. From getting an initial idea for a grant to researching the details and making a plan to finding funding sources, the book outlines the entire grant application process. Here, the novice will find advice on forming a grant-writing team, then actually writing, editing, and proofreading the proposal. The book offers grant submission tips and information on implementing the grant that results from a successful proposal.

Write Grants, Get Money, 2nd Edition offers many bonus features, including a CD. On the CD are copies of funded grants, examples of curricula vitae and resumes, and a PowerPoint® presentation on grant writing written by Dr. Gail Dickinson. Further resources in the text include a glossary, a bibliography, and an index.

Purpose

School librarians will find this book useful if they have never written a grant before, if they are veteran grant writers, or if they are somewhere in between. They'll find wisdom shared by school library media specialists from all over the United States who have written winning grant proposals and want to help their colleagues do the same.

A common characteristic of outstanding school librarians is a constant striving for more technology, better programming, more opportunities for their students, and more timely materials for the media center. This book will give the resourceful librarian the edge when applying for grant funding, and it can be used time and time again as a reference resource.

Long-Range Plan

The following chapters will help the reader develop a broad, comprehensive plan for the future of the media center and identify needs that might be met by grant money. The process of writing grants is complex and requires a long-term vision, commitment, and plan. The steps in the book will guide you as you develop your long-range plan and begin to write mini-grants and later as you write more complicated, larger grants. It will encourage the reader to become a grant reviewer in order to understand the grant-writing process and what makes a grant proposal succeed.

Grant-Writing Team

The book focuses on putting a grant-writing team together and then actually writing the grant. From reading the fine print to careful editing, the reader will find practical guidance on grant writing and proposal submission. Definitions and examples, or sources for examples, of the sections of a grant proposal are included. The reader will gain insight on what to do if the grant proposal is not funded and tips on how to proceed when the grant is funded.

This meat-and-potatoes approach will answer questions, furnish necessary resources, and inspire the reader to get started or continue writing winning grant proposals for the media center.

Write Grants, Get Money, 2nd Edition is not a dissertation, nor is it based on scholarly research. It is written from the experience of grant-writing practitioners studying in the school of hard knocks. The reader should feel free to experiment with the advice or methods suggested and make them his own. The authors are not professional grant writers nor do they have any plans to quit their day jobs. They are just educators who want to share the benefits that come from writing winning grant proposals.

Chapter *1*

Identify the Need

One who takes small steps goes fast.

— Anonymous

Picture Your Dream

Just like the little engine who thought she could, you have to think that you can
before you can. You have to dream big. Did you know that J.K. (Joanne Kathleen)
Rowling dreamed of writing a series of books about a kid named Harry Potter?

Her dream came true, in part,
through a grant from the
Scottish Arts Council.Grants
can be just the shot of energy
and resources you need to help
you know you can make a
difference for the students in
your media center and school.

Just like Alice in
Wonderland, you need to
dream six impossible things

before breakfast everyday. If you do not dream of the impossible, how can your dreams come true? Do not let the status quo limit your thinking. Do you dream of your students podcasting a weekly program about what is going on at school? If you can dream it for your students and your media center, it can come true.

But before your dream can come true, you have to identify it. Time spent dreaming the big dream for your library is time well spent. If you, like Harry Potter, had a magic media-center wand, what would you wish for? What is your "if dreams came true" vision for your media center? Let your imagination flow. Picture your ideal program and facility. How are students achieving? Is this true for all students? What does the facility look like? What resources and technology are available for your students and staff? To what heights could those test scores soar?

You will need to dream both broadly and specifically. You will need a clear vision of the big picture and also zoom shots of the specifics.

Use your school data to help you with your dream. See how students are achieving and then look at the school goals. What subject areas need more emphasis? What could your library program do to improve student reading scores? What could your library do to contribute to decreasing the drop-out rate for your students? This is important data for you to analyze as you picture great things for your library program. Consider involving your library advisory committee or the school improvement team in your planning.

You could cut pictures of your ideal equipment from catalogs and post them with magnets on your bulletin board or file cabinet. You could try writing a paragraph or two describing your dream. Consider buying yourself a journal and giving yourself permission to dream impossible dreams in it. Try using an artist's sketchbook from the art supply store. They do not have lines that make you feel compelled to fill all before turning the page. Embellish the cover with rubber stamps, quotes, and trinkets to personalize it. Jot down ideas, sketches, and short paragraphs about things you can envision for the future. It gives you a delicious feeling, rather like being a child and thinking of all the possibilities out there in the world.

Use the power of visualization. Let yourself dream; it's good for your spirit. Get those dreams written down somewhere, and make them reality.

Get Specific: Component Dreams

Once you have a mental picture of your big dream, you need to pull it apart into smaller component dreams and fill in the details. One of those components would make the perfect starting place for writing your first grant proposal. Apply for grants that target one or two specific goals or areas. Your chances will be better than if you start out asking for the moon. Later in your grant writing career you may tackle multi-year, complex federal grants, but we recommend keeping it simple to start.

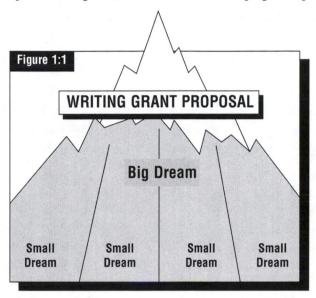

Figure 1:1
WRITING GRANT PROPOSAL
Big Dream
Small Dream   Small Dream   Small Dream   Small Dream

It's important to have the big picture dream, but keep in mind that writing a grant is a large undertaking and cannot be done in a day. It might even take an entire school year. Your big-picture dream may take a full career to accomplish, while one component of that dream may take only a school year to achieve.

Share Your Dream

Begin to seek support for your dream. Share your vision with your principal. Sharing with your principal or supervisor can be very helpful and should even be mandatory. First of all, she needs to be in your loop and support your dream. Second, if your principal or supervisor knows what you are dreaming, she can sometimes help you make your dream come true. Your principal may have capital funds remaining at the end of the budget year and might be willing to purchase a digital camcorder for the media center if she is aware that you want one. Or maybe she has enough for the editing software or carrying case you need. Every little bit of funding inches you forward toward your ideal program.

Share your vision with your colleagues. You never know who might be in a position to share your dream with someone who could connect you with a potential funding source. Bring your dream alive by having a planning session with your media center Dream Team. Your Dream Team could include your:

- library aide or clerk,
- interested and supportive teachers,
- parents,
- students,
- and library volunteers.

Your dream team may be your library advisory committee. Getting early buy-in is critical to the success of your long-range plan. Your team must be on the same page with you if you plan to reach for the stars together. Never underestimate the power of a team of educators with a clear mission.

If your principal or supervisor agrees with you, share your dream with students, staff, and parents. Build community support for your vision for your media center. You never know when opportunity might come knocking at your media center door. Keep a focus on improving student achievement and school climate.

Prepare for the Journey

Start keeping a journal in which you record your wishes and dreams for your media center. Allow yourself to be childlike in your journal. Do not let your grown-up self inhibit you. It does not matter if your dreams might be hard to achieve. What matters is that you give yourself license to brainstorm in an uncensored way. Carry your journal around with you, but do not share it with anyone who might rain on your parade.

Put it beside your bed at night, just in case your subconscious solves a logistics problem for you or comes up with an ace idea. You do not have to confine your dreams to just your media center, either. If you want to attend a summer institute in storytelling, put that in your journal. Professional development and professional growth opportunities have the potential to be funded by grants.

Visualize

Visualization is a powerful strategy. Try picturing yourself at the circulation desk with your new state-of-the-art check-out computer. Picture your high school students seated on those teak garden benches as they read periodicals in the new garden reading area of your library.

Cicero said, "Anyone who has a library and a garden wants for nothing." Like Don Quixote, dream the impossible dream.

Write a Mission Statement

Do you have a mission statement for your library? Does your school have a mission statement? One of the things you will need as you apply for your grant is a statement of beliefs or a mission statement. While you are dreaming about what you would like your library to be, start developing your mission statement. A mission statement is a simple statement expressing what you are about and what you want your library to be.

Start making notes in your journal. Write down words or phrases that express your ideals. After a few weeks of writing a note or two each day, take time to read what you have written and begin to edit. Your mission statement can be as short as one or two sentences that express succinctly what your library vision is all about.

Evening Star School Library Mission Statement

In the Evening Star School library we shall draw a circle and make sure that every student fits inside it. Regardless of race, gender, ability or background, each student will feel empowered to learn, thrive, read, research, and study in an energy-filled, technology-rich, supportive environment.

Start a Resume

If you don't have a current resume, begin making notes about your credentials. You will need a resume to include with your proposal or letters of inquiry. Where did you earn your college degrees and in what years? Where have you worked? What leadership positions have you held? Have you been PTA president or treasurer? What is your current job title and what are your duties and responsibilities? Get started writing a resume or curriculum vitae sheet that will tell the grant-makers who you are. See the accompanying CD for sample resumes of school library media specialists and other educators.

Think Outside the Book

Think outside the book when you are dreaming big for your library media center. What would your library program look like if you put project-based learning at the center of your lessons? What would the students be doing differently? What technology would you need to allow that to happen? How could you help your students take a more active role in their own learning? How could you help improve student scores? You may have some ideas that you have not seen in practice before. That is okay. That is what makes one grant proposal stand out against another. Unique ideas, presented in a colorful way, may be just what it takes to get your grant funded.

When you think about writing a grant, have no fear. At least, have little fear. You have hard-earned degrees, you have written substantive research papers, and you teach people how to do research. You can write a winning grant proposal. There is money there for the asking. You can do it! So get started.

Developing a comprehensive, long-range plan for your media center is worth your while. Many school districts have long-range plans. Check to see if yours does. If so, study your district's long range plan and model your library plan from that. Does your school have a school improvement plan? If so, study that as well and model your library plan from your school's improvement plan. What are the school goals? Are they to improve student achievement in reading and math? Is there a school goal to reduce drop-out rates? If so, those are appropriate goals for you to include in your long-range library plan.

There are several areas in your library that you could consider when you are looking at a long-range dream/plan. Several facets of your program and facility have potential for enhancements. Start by analyzing student achievement data. In what reading areas are your students scoring well and in what areas do they need help? If scores are weak in interpreting text features, then you might make a plan to develop your collection with more current nonfiction books that include glossaries, indexes, tables of content, illustrations with captions, and other text features. Maybe you need a projector in your library classroom that you can use to teach text features in your library classes. Once you have identified the needs in your student scores and made a long-range plan for improving them—working of course with your colleagues—it is time to read journal articles, take field trips, attend conferences, and visit with colleagues for ideas to help solve the problems, increase the scores, and reduce the drop-out rate.

What About Library Technology?

E-Rate

One of the first steps you may want to take is to find out if your school district has a long-range technology plan. If your district has ever sought E-rate funding, there is probably an existing technology plan because that is one of the requirements to qualify for E-rate. See if you can find that technology plan and read it. It may include your school district's vision for the future of technology in your library, in your school, and in your district.

E-rate is a federal fund to help schools and libraries get affordable access to the Internet. For more information about E-rate, visit <http://www.edlinc.org>.

Technology Plan

Consider developing a long-range district technology plan if you don't already have one. To write a district-wide technology plan, you'll need to involve your superintendent and other administrators. If a committee is forming to write or update your district technology plan, volunteer to serve on it. Not only will you have a chance to give your input, you will see from the beginning what the long-range dreams are for your schools.

Make your long-range technology vision specific so that you are ready to act when you have the opportunity. Take inventory of what you have; then you can make a long-range plan for computer replacement. A sample technology inventory sheet for you to use is included on the accompanying CD.

As you make your long-range plan, prioritize your wishes and estimate the school year during which you would like to acquire the equipment. Although you may not be able to replace all your technology with grant money, you will not have wasted your effort by making a technology replacement plan. You may be in the right place at the right time if you have done your homework, prioritized your needs, and made a timeline for replacement and enhancement of your technology. Keep that long-range technology plan current.

Web 2.0

There are probably technology needs that you have in order to use Web 2.0 technology in your library. This seems an obvious and fruitful place to design a plan to enhance your library. What do your students need in order to produce hands-on projects using the latest in Web 2.0 methods? Podcasting equipment, maybe, if you don't already have it?

Cautions

As you put together a plan for technology, observe a few cautions:
- Seek help when you need it.
- Build budget room in your proposal for price changes.
- Build in funds for forgotten cables, tapes, and the like.
- Make sure hardware and software are compatible.
- Follow district and state guidelines about purchasing, once you have your funds.
- Consider building in funds for installation, maintenance, and ongoing licenses.
- Go see what you are requesting before you request it.
- Make sure you have the required power, data drops and/or wireless connections.
- Ask questions and take the advice of experts.

Needs Other Than Technology

Technology is not the only game in grant-writing town. Consider other areas as you envision your ideal library.

Collection Development

Do you need to acquire a variety of materials about cultural diversity? Is there a Rainbow Coalition in your community that funds efforts to promote understanding and harmony in your neighborhood or city? Your need to acquire multicultural materials may match their mission. Call them and see what grant monies might be available. Focus on making your media center a culturally inclusive mecca in your school.

Are you planning to offer e-books to your patrons? What about MP3 players with books already loaded on them? How will you fund that? Tell your principal about your ideas. Do you have special collections—other languages, diversity, special needs, classroom collections, or historic archives—that might be enhanced by a grant?

Handicapped Accessibility

Do you need funding to bring your media center into compliance with the Americans with Disabilities Act? Does your school need an elevator so that all students can access the library? Do you lack computer tables and other furniture that is accessible from a wheelchair? Need a new circulation desk or modifications to the present one to make it wheelchair-accessible?

Special Programs

Consider writing a grant proposal for:

- A program to serve young mothers,
- After-school activities,
- Before and after-school tutoring,
- Family reading, science, or math night in the library,
- Multicultural events, or
- Mentoring programs.

Facility Needs

Do your younger students need a reading loft? Does your school need a faculty work area in the library for teachers who, because of space constraints, cannot be in their classrooms during their planning periods? An educational software company's foundation might be interested in funding such a project.

Furniture

Would a rocking chair make your story area more appealing? Do you need to replace your board-and-brick makeshift shelving with sturdy new shelving? Furniture needs to consider:

- Shelving,
- Circulation desk,
- Tables and chairs,
- Lounge furniture,
- Media storage equipment, and
- Computer furniture.

Environment and School Climate

Start with a goal to make the school climate inclusive for all students and staff. What would you need for that goal? For some dynamic ideas, read *The Power of the Media Specialist to Improve Academic Achievement and Strengthen at-Risk Students* by Jones and Zambone (Linworth Publishing, Inc., 2008).

Perhaps there's a feng shui expert on staff who wants to give you sage advice on increasing the harmony, learning, and circulation in your library, or maybe your library just needs a face-lift. Your local home decorating center may be your fairy godmother. Do you need a coat of paint or do you need the whole nine yards of new blinds, paint, and carpet? Do you want lamps for ambient lighting or display cases to highlight student projects or artwork? Would a drinking fountain improve concentration and increase traffic? Here are some furnishings to consider:

- Display cases,
- Artwork,
- Lamps and other lighting,
- Blinds or shades,
- Flooring, and
- Paint or wall treatment.

Memorials

When a community has lost a well-loved teacher, student, or parent, they wish to pay some lasting tribute to that person. The library is well suited to house a memorial, and grant money can be a way to provide it.

Workshops

Maybe your budget will buy books for your library but won't cover special events like an author visit. Apply for a grant to fund your next staff, student, or visiting author workshop. Depending on the cost of your dream event, you may need more than one money source.

To host visiting authors, many school districts supplement their budgets with donations—both monetary or goods and services—from their PTA or local banks, bakeries, bookstores, hotels, and other businesses. They finance large, expensive events with several donations from various sources. Rarely is there a Daddy Warbucks who will fund an entire workshop. But the local baker may bake you a cake for your author reception and the neighborhood restaurant provide a complimentary dinner. Generous community members might be willing to support a program beneficial to young people.

Are your creative juices flowing? Do you have the skeleton of a plan in your mind for a grant proposal for your library? From that skeleton of an idea, make an outline and try to put some flesh on the bones of an award-winning grant proposal for your media center to benefit your students.

Getting Started

As you prepare to write your grant proposal, continue to fill in the details of the long-range plan/vision for your media center. Get to the store and buy that little spiral notebook in which you can jot down your ideas as they pop into your brain. As ideas come to you, try to follow the rules of brainstorming by thinking of all the possibilities that you can for your media center. Do not edit your ideas for feasibility, spelling, and correct grammar—just brainstorm. Keep the notebook close at hand. You never know when the flash of a good idea is going to hit you. Good ideas sometimes pop up at the least expected times and places. A pocket-sized voice recorder might be just the ticket for those good ideas that need to be captured.

As you think of them, add the names of the people you need to talk with and make a list of the field trips and site visits you need to make. Remember, a good idea is at the heart of every successful grant, so do not let one slip by without making a record of it. You can refine and embellish it later.

Leonardo da Vinci kept journals or notebooks beside him. He sketched in them, wrote down ideas as they came to him, and drew diagrams of potential projects and ideas. The way we see it, if Leonardo thought it was a good idea, who are we to criticize? If a spreadsheet is more your cup of tea, start a spreadsheet of grant information.

Next, you must fill in some of the details of your dream before it can become reality. For example, if you want the equipment needed to podcast in your library, gather information about exactly what you need. Once you know that, log onto manufacturers' Web sites to research what type of microphone and Web camera you should get, how much they cost, and what the specifications for them are. Print out the information you find. Start a document or a spreadsheet on your computer and then record the data about the podcasting equipment in it. You have now started the budget section of a grant proposal. You are in business!

Enter a Contest

Contests are a great place to cut your grant-writing teeth. Enter any contests you can that might provide recognition for your students, staff, school, or media center. Any time you can bring positive recognition to your school and media center, it's a step toward your objective. Winning contests and honors fortifies your credibility with funding sources. And in the process of entering contests, you are learning and practicing the skills of writing a winning entry. Just to get you started try some of the sites listed in Appendix I as you look for contest, awards, and grants.

Think Solid, Not Earthshaking

Keep in mind that the idea you start to embellish for a grant proposal does not have to be earthshaking or profound. You simply need a good, solid idea that is going to make a difference in student learning, achievement, or understanding. It is fine to take an idea that you have read about or seen somewhere and modify it for your setting. You don't have to come up with a wholly original idea, just one that you can embellish and modify to fit your library and benefit your students and staff.

Strive for Action, Not Perfection

Remember that your goal is to get started on a simple grant request project, not to write the Pulitzer Prize-winning grant of all time. Use the strategy of taking an action, no matter how small, every day to build your grant-writing momentum. Make a phone call; participate in a Webinar; explore an Internet site devoted to grants. E-mail a media specialist from a neighboring district and see if he knows about any available grants. Read a technology journal while looking for grant opportunities. Find someone who blogs about grants and sign up for an RSS feed. Start or revise your resume. Write a paragraph describing your mission for your library. You can revise it later. Don't strive for perfection. Just take action. Do something.

Get the show on the road. The people who get grant money are the people who apply for it. Many people have good ideas for grants, but the only people who will ever get the grants are ones who apply. Do not let fear of failure keep you from taking action. Get up and boogie! Getting money is a function of persistence and discipline.

Project Objectives

At the same time you are planning the various possible grant projects, you also need to focus on your objectives. Decide what you want to accomplish with your grant project and then spell out your objectives in a measurable way. Don't forget, the No. 1 best way to show progress is with student achievement. Once you have some clear, measurable goals, you will be able to see how your project fits with the goals of your potential benefactor.

Grant proposal writing is a fluid process. While you are writing one proposal, you may have other projects in the idea development stage. Keep in motion; keep the momentum going.

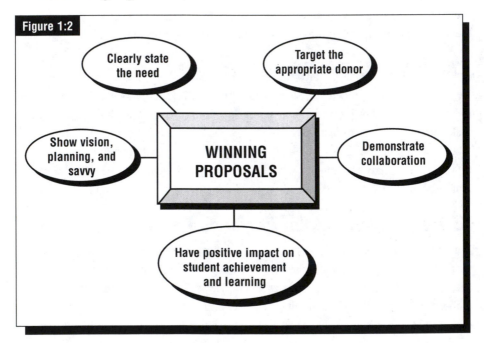

Figure 1:2

Clearly state the need

Target the appropriate donor

Show vision, planning, and savvy

WINNING PROPOSALS

Demonstrate collaboration

Have positive impact on student achievement and learning

- Stop now and get your first few ducks in a row. You've begun to dream your dream and it's time to get started.
- Start keeping your journal to note ideas to consider, people to interview.
- Begin your research by visiting other media centers and exploring relevant Web resources.
- Get others involved by talking with your principal, other administrators, key teachers, your library advisory committee, and community members.
- Focus on the positive impact your grant could have on student learning and achievement.

Chapter 2

Go Where the Grants Are

Research is the act of going up alleys to see if they are blind.

— Plutarch

Picture in your mind those specially trained truffle pigs in France. You know, the ones who can sniff out truffles that no one can see buried in the ground? Our goal is to be grant sniffers—extraordinaire!

Where shall we start? Multiple funding sources are waiting to be tapped for our media centers. Our job is to be good detectives and find those sources, and after that, to become marketing experts to sell our vision and our need for funding it to the right grantor.

In the world of grant-making, there are private, corporate, and government sources at the local, state, and federal level that have funds to award. The trick is

to make a good match. Let's position you to be at the right place at the right time so that you can make a match with the ideal grantor. See examples of potential fund sources at the end of the chapter.

One of your most important jobs as you begin to shop for grant money is to learn about the mission or goals of prospective benefactors. Grant makers have a passionate desire to solve social problems and eliminate inequities in society. They want to fund projects that advance their goals.

You also need to learn about prospective benefactors' patterns of giving. Do they award grants in your locale? What kinds of grants have they awarded recently and to whom? What are their application deadlines?

As you prepare to write your grant proposal and market your program to benefactors, keep these questions in mind:

- What are the benefits for the funding organization if they fund my grant?
- What is the funding organization's mission?
- Where does the grant maker's vision intersect with my program's goals?
- How can I market my project to appeal to this entity?

Organize Your Research

Good research practice can help you find funding sources that match the profile of your needs and dreams. Librarians are the best researchers on the earth, so this can be one of the easier tasks you face. You will need to keep good records and be organized as you search for sponsors. While a potential grantor might not fit your current project, he might be a perfect prospect for your next project.

Three-by-five index cards work to record your data if you don't want to use a spreadsheet. Use colored index cards to indicate the type of money source—one color for federal agencies, another for private foundations, and a third for community foundations. If you jot the name of the foundation, the address, contact person, information about projects they fund, and Web site address, you can build a colorful file of potential funding sources.

You may prefer to start a spreadsheet or database and enter your data directly into it. Either way, the important thing is to gather the information and keep track of it in an organized manner for easy retrieval. Whatever method you choose, this file will be a building block in your grant-seeking program. Keep it current.

Some Tips

Stay Flexible. It is common for corporate foundations to have unstructured grant application processes. In one way this can make your effort easier because you do not need to write such a formal grant proposal. On the other hand, since the guidelines are not as clear, it can make it more difficult to try to hit the target with your proposal.

Make Contacts. It can be helpful if you know someone in a corporation. Corporations tend to support organizations with which they already have a working relationship. Does your school have a corporate partner? If so, that would be a reasonable organization to explore as you seek a grant sponsor.

If you know someone in a corporation, you might be able to gain some pertinent information. Ask about any potential grant money the company might have and what its goals are for spending this money. Begin to build a relationship with potential donors. Learn the phone number and name of the secretary to the person in charge of corporate giving. Add that information to your index card or database for future reference.

Be kind and professional to each person you speak with at the organization. Good manners go a long way. You never know who the informal leaders in an organization are. Your kindness to the executive secretary may be remembered months later when your grant proposal arrives in the mail.

Start Close to Home. Before writing a formal grant proposal to a foundation as you search for funding, you might consider seeking funding from a local corporation or business. Local businesses can be excellent sources for funding in the community. Seeking funding from a local business is an excellent, low-risk way for you to start your fund-raising career.

Do you want to reward your student library volunteers with an end-of-the-year breakfast? Write up your plan and take it to the manager of the grocery store where your school families shop. Asking for orange juice and bagels for 10 students is a great way to start your grant-writing career. If your grocer supports your request, you have your first "grant"—almost painlessly.

At the volunteer breakfast, credit the grocer. Thank her in your parent newsletter and send a copy of the published article with your thank-you note. Make bookmarks for your volunteers with a credit line on them to the grocer and include one of those in your letter. Sing the grocer's praises at the next PTA meeting. Write a letter to the Chamber of Commerce saluting the grocer. Make your grocer feel proud of his or her generosity. Give credit where credit is due.

You will find there are many local and national groups that offer funding or prizes for special projects. The Daughters of the American Revolution (DAR) and Sertoma International are two such groups in many communities that have assisted media specialists.

Types of Grants

Foundations

Various kinds of foundations may have funding available for your media center.

- **Independent or Private Foundations** frequently fund public television and radio programs; you'll see or hear their names among the credits at the end. There are about 50,000 private foundations in the United States, many founded by prosperous families who support arts and humanities or other special interests. Researching their interests and grant criteria is important preliminary work for crafting your grant request. A majority of family foundations limit their funding to their local community. No sense in applying for funding for your Kansas media center when the foundation funds projects only in Mississippi. You will learn this information in your research. Don't forget to note the foundation's special interests on your index card or in your database.

- **The Ezra Jack Keats Foundation** is an example of a foundation that offers mini-grants for innovative programs that combat illiteracy in public schools. For information about these mini-grants, contact Executive Director, Ezra Jack Keats Foundation, 450 14th St., Brooklyn, NY 11215. <www.ezra-jack-keats.org/programs/minigrant.html>

- **Company-Sponsored Foundations** usually fund projects relating to the company's interests, often exclusively in the locale or regions where the company operates. Corporate foundations typically fund projects that will enhance the corporate image, provide a benefit to their employees, make the community more valuable to the corporation, or help the company reach corporate goals. Corporate Web sites offer information about these foundations. One of your jobs as you research and plan your project is to figure out how your goals for your media center fit with the company's goals.

  For example, 3M offers Professional Development Grants each year. Library recipients are chosen from national applicants. The grants are given to American Library Association's New Members Round Table (NMRT) and are called 3M/NMRT Professional Development Grants. Recipients are chosen for their activism in the association, their commitment to librarianship, and their career development goals. For more information about the grants, contact 3M or check out the ALA Web site at <www.ala.org>.

- **Community Foundations** work with individuals, corporations, and other non-profit organizations to fund projects in the local area. Your city or county may have a community foundation whose mission is congruent with yours.

Government Funds

Many government agencies have grant money they are charged with awarding. The art is to find which agency grants funds for your type of project and then to meet the complex qualifications and guidelines of a government grant. If you are allergic to red tape, don't start your grant-writing career by applying for a government grant. The process is comparable to taking an upper-level graduate course. Start by applying to a smaller grantor successfully before tackling a government grant. When you have the experience of writing a winning grant application or two, you are ready to try for the big bucks of a government grant. Work with a team if you plan to apply for a government grant because of its complexity and the research and diligence it will require.

The government publishes *The Grant Award Actions Database* for you to access online at <http://Web99.ed.gov/grant/grtawd00.nsf> This is a one-stop source of extensive information on all the current year's Education Department (ED) grants.

The following are some of the types of government grants:

- *Library Services and Construction Act (LSCA)* grants are given to state libraries, earmarked for specific types of library projects. Each state has its own rules and regulations for awarding funds, but they are all governed by federal legislation. Request the *LSCA Handbook* from your state library for information about the kinds of proposals your state funds. There are many restrictions, so read the regulations carefully.

- *Library Services and Technology Act (LSTA)* Special Populations grants are open to libraries of all types. To learn more about them, send a letter of intent to your state library and request an application and guidelines.

- *National Endowment for the Humanities (NEH)* was set up by Congress to support research and education projects in the humanities. If you are interested in pursuing NEH funding, be sure to seek assistance at <http://www.neh.fed.us/>. NEH has very high standards. Consider working with a professor from a local college or university if you are seriously pursuing NEH funding. You may need the research, expertise, and experience of a past recipient to compete in this league.

NEH offers a publication entitled *Humanities Projects in Libraries and Archives: Guidelines and Application Instructions*. This document can be ordered from NEH, Division of Public Programs. It is item number OMB #3136-0118.

The American Library Association (ALA) works in conjunction with NEH on some projects. For more information about ALA's humanities program, see its publications or use the information at <http://www.ala.org/alaorg/staff/staff.html> to contact the ALA director of public programs.

- **State Humanities Councils** fund a variety of projects. If you are seeking funding for a visiting author or a writer's workshop, this might be a venue for you. You will find a bibliography of state arts and humanities councils in Appendix F of this book.

Resources to Help Find Grantors
Internet Searches

When you use keyword searches for grant money, you will have many hits. Use basic Boolean operators of "and," "or," and "not" to get closer to finding exactly what you want.

Another way to research is to search the Internet for specific technology manufacturers' Web sites and look for any foundations they might have established. It is possible to spend hours on the Internet searching for potential grant funds. The harvest of prospective donors is usually huge and will give you plenty of data to sift through.

- **RightGrant Online** is a free school grant locating service at <www.teachersuniverse.com>.

- **The Foundation Center** is a service organization that helps grant seekers find information about potential donors. Foundation Center libraries are located at several sites around the country and at <http://www.fdncenter.org>.

- **The Council on Foundations** <http://www.cof.org/links> keeps information on independent foundations.

- **Catalog of Federal Domestic Assistance (CFDA)** is a U.S. government publication available from the Superintendent of Documents, Washington, DC 20402 or at <http://www.cfda.gov/>.

- **The Federal Register** is a daily government publication, also available from the Superintendent of Documents, that will keep you posted on federal grant application deadlines, rules, and regulations. Access it online at <http://www.access.gpo.gov/su_docs/aces/aces140.html>.

Directories

Several foundation directories are available at your local community library, the nearby college library, or at one of the Foundation Center libraries. Some school districts have grant writing personnel or offices that may own these resources, too. These directories will lead you to foundations, their guidelines, annual reports, contact information, and other pertinent data.

- **Corporate 500: The Directory of Corporate Philanthropy** is a comprehensive directory of funding information published by Public Management Institute, San Francisco, California. ISBN # 0916664580.

- **Corporate Giving Directory** includes sample grant recipients. Taft Group in Detroit, Michigan, publishes it. ISBN# 1569954046.

- **The Foundation Directory**, published in New York by the Foundation Center, is your source for information about some of the largest foundations in the country. ISBN# 087959440.

- **The Foundation Directory, Part 2**, also published by the Foundation Center, has information on mid-sized foundations that make grants from $25,000 to $100,000. ISBN# 0879549459.

- **Foundation Grants to Individuals**, published by the Foundation Center, lists foundations that make grants of $2,000 or more to individuals. ISBN# 0879543876.

- **Statistical Abstract of the United States, 2000: The National Data Book** lists foundations with less than $1 million in assets that make grants of $100,000 or more. It is published in Austin, Texas, by Hoover's Business Press. ISBN#1573110639.

- **The National Directory of Corporate Giving**, published by the Foundation Center, has excellent information on funding sources. ISBN# 0879548886.

Journal, Blog, and Newsletter Searching

Start scouring the library, technology journals, e-journals, Web sites, blogs, and newsletters for current grant opportunities. Look for the columns entitled *Grant Awards* and *Grant Deadlines*. Look in *Cable in the Classroom, e-School News, Learning and Leading with Technology, Library Media Connection, net connect* (supplement to *Library Journal* and *School Library Journal*), *Technology Today*, and other educational technology journals.

You probably already read school library professional journals. Watch carefully for notices of grant opportunities in columns in *American Library, Knowledge Quest, Library Journal, Library Media Connection, Horn Book, School Library Journal, Voice of Youth Advocates,* and others. Make it your habit to check the journals every month for current grant information. You may see nothing of interest for six months and then hit the jackpot in the seventh month.

Sign up for RSS feeds for some of your favorite blogs and watch for notifications or discussions of grants and potential funders. You may also find people with whom to collaborate as you read and respond to blogs and library discussion groups on Moodle.

Keep your eye out for those truffles! Don't lose faith in finding a good match for your needs.

Search Tips

- ***Write or Call for Application Forms and Guidelines.*** A first step in writing a grant proposal to a private foundation is to go online and download the application forms. The addresses and URLs for most foundations can be found online. Once you receive the information, start a file folder for that foundation and file it in your Potential Donors file. You may need an accordion file for the annual reports and the file folders you have established for each foundation. The annual reports are informative but usually hefty. Hanging files will also work well for bulky reports.

- ***Contact Past Grantees.*** If you can learn from the foundation or from your research the name of someone who has received a grant from this foundation, contact that person and learn more about the grant, the process, and the winning proposal. Educators are happy and eager to share their victories with colleagues. There are no better team players on the earth than educators, so make a call and learn from someone else's experience.

- ***Build Relationships.*** Once you have found potential donors, you need to begin to establish relationships with them. A simple act of courtesy, such as clipping the picture of someone you know in the paper who is on the board of the local DAR, can help you make a connection. Cut the picture out and send it to the board member with a thoughtful note. Begin simply to establish connections. Build a bridge between you, your program, and potential supporters.

  There is grant money out there. You can find and claim some for your library. It is well within your reach.

- ***Network.*** Sometimes, the fastest and easiest way to find a grantor is to network with your colleagues to learn who has gotten grants from whom. Go fishin'! Ask your neighboring media specialists; ask the public librarians. Ask your favorite listserv. Ask your sorority or fraternity associates, your professional association, and the staff at the nearby school of library information management. Someone you know can tell you where there is grant money available and waiting for you. Jot down the sources you hear about in your spiral notebook or spreadsheet.

- ***Send a Query Letter.*** When you find a potential grantor, a solid next step is to send a query letter telling about your idea and explaining its merits. This is a little like dangling bait in the water of the grant pool. Make it short, upbeat, and to the point.

Describe your plan in one paragraph. You probably will be inquiring about one of your component dreams, not your big-picture dream, so it should be easy to describe quickly and succinctly.

State the reason for your request and a ballpark figure for the amount of funding you will need. Include a needs statement, the target population, and some statistics. Request a funding application. Be sure to include the granting organization's name, title, and address, and direct it to the appropriate person. Also include a brief profile of your school.

If you feel it would be appropriate, request a list of past grantees and reviewers to be included in your packet. If that does not seem appropriate, request general information on the types of reviewers they use–their backgrounds, professions, and criteria on which they are selected. If all the reviewers are educators, it might make a difference in how you write your grant. If you knew that some of the reviewers were noneducators, you would definitely be more careful about using common education jargon.

Once you have received that information, contact a past grantee, if you can. Introduce yourself, explain how you got her name, and ask some questions that may help you as you write your grant proposal.

For an example, contact a consultant who has worked with several state departments of education. She could give you good advice for new grant writers like: Focus on what you want to fund. Set a well-defined goal. Before you begin writing, involve anyone who will be collaborating with you, such as administration, legal counsel, and teachers. Be succinct. Tell what you're going to do, how you'll do it, how you'll measure it, and what it will cost. In the grant proposal writer's opinion, the hardest part about writing grants is first deciding what you want to do and then getting people to buy in to your plan once you've started the process. Grantees like this know what they are talking about. They get millions of dollars of grant money, sometimes on the third or fourth try.

- *Use Listservs and Blogs for School Librarians.* Listservs are a convenient and economical way to network with others who have the same or similar jobs to yours. You can learn what grants others in your trade have received and what tips they may have for you. You can bounce your proposal ideas off colleagues and get their feedback. You can also be a listserv lurker, one who subscribes and reads the postings but doesn't respond. If you are shy, you may find lurking a comfortable way to enter the world of listservs. See Appendix H for listservs. Another good source of information can be found on school library special interest blogs. Find one or two that you enjoy reading that have occasional information on grant money, grant writing, and funders. Sign up for an RSS feed to keep you posted.

- *Go Back to School.* Some colleges and universities offer a graduate level course in grant writing. If you are seeking additional graduate credits, see if your local college or university offers a grant-writing course. Maybe you can learn more about grant writing and get graduate credit at the same time.

Another educational option is to attend a workshop or seminar in grant writing. There are full or half-day seminars offered by national presenters. It is also possible to contact a presenter who will design a seminar or workshop in grant writing specifically for your faculty or school district and will conduct it at your location.

A third educational option is to take a Web-based course. Sites such as Grantswriters.com at <http://grantwriters.com/training.htm> offer interactive online courses in grant writing. This is a convenient option for those who live far from a college campus but want to enroll in a course.

- **Consult Journals, E-journals, and Print Media.** In the bibliography of this book you will find several journals that have regular columns announcing upcoming grant competitions and their submission dates. Many books have been written on grant writing, and each has suggestions for finding potential donors.

- **Search the Web.** It's a great way to find potential funding sources. See the bibliography in this book for some suggestions. You can subscribe to online databases that track grant and foundation funding information. For instance, the *GRANTS Database,* available online through Dialog and through Knowledge Express Data Systems, identifies approximately 9,000 public and private programs that make grants. Find ordering information online at <http://www.oryxpress.com/order.htm>.

- **Learn from Professional Organizations and Neighbors.** The American Library Association, the American Association of School Librarians, academic fraternities, and other professional associations, such as the National Education Association (NEA) and the Association for Curriculum and Development (ASCD), have information about funding sources for you. Most of these organizations have Web sites that display information on grant funding opportunities.

Visit media specialists in neighboring schools. Ask questions. See how others are solving the problems with which you are wrestling. Your colleagues can be excellent resources for you.

As you search for potential donors, you will see that you need to modify your dream to fit the requirements of the grant-making entity. Finding potential grant sources is an ongoing endeavor. You need to keep your grant-writing ear to the ground. Finding a benefactor is a little like finding the right job. You want to find an organization whose mission and goals are compatible with your own. Scouring Web sites, directories, and annual reports to learn more about the grant sources is one way to find a match for you and your vision.

- **Attend Conferences.** There are many good ideas at the national AASL conference or your state or regional library conferences. Sessions and presenters can be gold mines of best practices and great ideas. Listen to the presenters. Ask questions. Talk to the vendors. Who has seen projects worth reproducing? Attend the sessions on grant writing and learn from both the presenter and the participants.

  Attending a conference devoted solely to grant writing is an excellent option, if you can afford it. Technology groups such as *eSchool News* online sponsor meaningful conferences. *Grants & Funding for School Technology: A Strategic Conference for K-12 School Leaders* is a conference sponsored by *eSchool News* online. For information about it, go to <http://www.eschoolnews.org/>.

  If you live in or near a large city, you'll find many opportunities to attend grant-writing seminars. In Boston, for instance, the Foundation Center sponsors grant-writing workshops. Technical Development Corporation, the Center for Nonprofit Management at Boston Center for Adult Education, and the School of Management and Administrative Services at Lesley College also sponsor workshops in Boston. Search the web to see if there are similar opportunities in your town.

- **Collect Annual Reports.** Log on to a foundation's Web site or write a letter and request an annual report. There is nothing like an annual report to give you the real scoop on a foundation or corporation. You will see how the organization portrays itself and what its priorities are. Reading the annual report helps you know your potential grantor much better.

  Highlight language that you may want to include somewhere in your grant proposal. We all love to hear our favorite words and phrases repeated back to us. Reading some of his or her own words in your proposal is sure to impress the prospective donor favorably.

  File the annual reports and save them for future projects. While the grant you are seeking right now may not involve technology, your next one might. Hang on to that IBM annual report.

- **Cultivate a State Ally.** Personnel at the state department of education and at the state library are good contacts. Call someone at those agencies and describe to her the plan for which you are seeking funding. See if the state person knows where there might be funding for your project. She can give you feedback, cheer you on, point you in another direction, give you good advice, and even call you when a new request for proposal (RFP) comes through that sounds like a match to your project. Your state library contact might even be willing to collaborate with you in writing a grant proposal.

  While you have a state department of education person on the phone line, ask him to refer you to a past recipient of a grant of the type you are seeking. Give that recipient a call and see if she will give you guidance, suggestions, or advice.

  If your proposal is intriguing and you have visited with the proper people at the state level, you may be asked to submit a full proposal. But remember, just because you were encouraged to submit a proposal doesn't mean your grant will be funded. There are miles to go before you achieve that goal.

If you are asked to submit a full proposal, stay in touch with your state contact. Don't be pushy, but your contact might be willing to read your final draft before you submit it and give you tips. As you progress in writing the sections of your grant, check in with your contact when you have questions.

Start Your Search Close to Home

Start close to home and find out as much as you can about potential funding sources. Find an up-to-date directory of foundations for your area or state. Seek help from the librarian at your local library to find a foundation directory. Think about planning a field trip to the nearest Foundation Center Library, or at least check out the Foundation Center's Web site at <http://fdncenter.org/onlib/index.html> to learn the site nearest to you.

Be sure to use current reference materials as you shop for foundations and grant-givers. Beware of outdated directories. You could spin your wheels pursuing funding from a defunct foundation or one that no longer offers grants.

Knowing someone on the board of a local foundation or corporation is also helpful as you begin your grant-writing career. If you have a contact within the offices of a potential donor, find out what you can about the kinds of projects for which the organization typically awards grants. Seek guidance from those in the know. Remember, you are not looking for insider trading information, just helpful tips for finding a potential grant source and writing a winning grant proposal. Ask if you may see a copy of a project that was funded last year. You don't know until you ask—but be sure not to make a nuisance of yourself. Many foundation offices are run on a shoestring and often manned with volunteer help only.

At this point in your project you should:

- Organize your research;
- Consider the type of grant you wish to seek—federal, private, or other;
- Explore your search resources such as the Internet, directories, special libraries, and journals;
- E-mail, write, or call for forms and guidelines;
- Connect with potential grantors;
- Send a query letter;
- Join a listserv;
- See Appendix A for a list of possible funders;
- Take a grant proposal writing class;
- Attend a conference; and
- Order annual reports.

Chapter 3

Read Grants and Form a Writing Team

Two dogs will kill a lion.

— Hebrew Proverb

Be a Grant Reader

Make it a high priority to become a grant reader. It's one of the best ways to learn to write winning grant proposals. If your school district or parish is lucky enough to have support from a foundation, volunteer to be on the team that reads grant applications. The group of readers will probably be small, friendly, and eager to help you learn to sort the worthy from the unsuccessful grant proposals.

Do you know someone who reviews grants? If so, call and ask questions:

- How did you get started reading grants?
- Do you review grant proposals by mail or in meetings with other panelists?
- Can you describe some of the scoring systems you have used?
- Would you be willing to give me feedback on my grant proposal when it's written?
- What mistakes do you typically encounter in the proposals you read?
- How much time do you devote to proposal reading, and how many proposals do you normally read per grant?

Send your resume or curriculum vitae with a cover letter to organizations expressing interest in having you review grants for them. Highlight your credentials in your letter to the chair of the review committee. See the accompanying CD for sample resumes and curricula vitae.

Contest Judge

Another possible forum for you is to volunteer to serve on the committees that select contest winners. Typically your state or local professional organization recognizes outstanding media specialists. Volunteer to serve on that state committee. Volunteer to be on the scholarship committee for the American Library Association <http://www.ala.org>, for the American Association of School Librarians <http://www.ala.org/aasl/>, or for the International Reading Association at <http://www.reading.org/>.

Watch for the "Call for Nominations: Council, Committee Applications Available" column in *American Libraries*. The columnist recommends that your letter of application or nomination include professional qualifications and the name of the committee for which you are volunteering or nominating someone. Try the Web site at <https://cs.ala.org/rettig/volunteer.html>.

Some library vendors sponsor contests to honor librarians. Contact Follett, Scholastic, Gale, or another library product vendor who sponsors contests.

If you are chosen to sit on a selection committee, you will gain insight into how others market themselves and what attributes the grantors are seeking. You'll learn some "do's" and "don'ts" of proposal writing. You'll learn insider tips on what wins points and friends and what turns the judges off. The "don'ts" are just as important as the "do's" when you are learning marketing strategies for your media center and yourself.

Believe it or not, serving on the committees who read those applications will hone your skills for writing and for identifying a winning proposal. You will see applications that are concise, colorful, and congruent with the goals of the contest. Transfer those skills to writing grant proposals, and you will be in the winners' circle soon.

Reviewing Grants

When you are invited to review grants you will be asked to follow the review criteria of the funding organization. You will evaluate the strength and scope of the proposal; the credentials, past history, and credibility of the personnel who will be implementing the grant; the accuracy and thoroughness of the budget; and the overall impact of the proposed project.

You will be asked to write meaningful comments on each of the requests you read. The grantor will read these and may share with the proposal writer upon request. So be specific, meaningful, fair, and grammatically correct. Do not depend on spell-checker for correct spelling, either; keep your dictionary handy and use it.

Each funding entity and each grant competition may have its own set of criteria. In general, you will find that a specified number of points are possible in each section of the proposal. We will look at each of those sections in depth in a later chapter.

Reviewing Grants for Local Foundations

If you have foundations in your community, e-mail one of them and volunteer to read grant proposals for them. Even if they are not affiliated in any way with school library media centers, the experience will help you by familiarizing you with the format of a grant proposal and the qualities that make for a winning proposal. It doesn't matter, as you are learning to write proposals, whether the ones you are reading are education-related or not. The formats will be similar as will be the critical attributes of winning proposals.

Many school districts have education foundations that support them. If your school district is interested in enlisting outside support for innovative projects, think about forming an educational foundation. It is a relatively simple process to form a foundation, and the rewards are great. For an article on forming educational foundations go to <http://www.fno.org/fnosept91.html>.

Foundations formed specifically to support innovation in school districts are prime examples of potential grantors for media specialists. A school librarian who designs a project and writes a winning proposal to fund it can have a wide impact on his students, school, and community.

For an example of a foundation established to support the Shawnee Mission (Kansas) School District, see the CD. There you will see a brochure soliciting grant proposals for the Shawnee Mission Education Foundation. You will also see support information for an amazing fund drive to update the libraries. Visit the foundation online at <http://www.smef.org> to gain an idea of the type of grant competitions organized by education foundations.

Reviewing State Grants

Your state department of education probably uses grant-reading teams to select recipients of state grants. E-mail the person who assembles these teams and volunteer to serve on one. Send her your curriculum vitae electronically with a letter stating your interest. Don't be disappointed if you are not selected on your first try, but continue to volunteer until you are chosen to read. Also, let your boss know you'd like to be on a proposal-reading team. He may be able to recommend you.

When you are selected to serve on a proposal review team, you will be asked to take a pledge of confidentiality, a critical value in proposal review. Never tell anyone but your supervisor that you are serving on a grant review team.

Once chosen to read grants, you'll typically be mailed 10 to 20 grant proposals to read by a certain date, along with a scoring rubric and specific directions for reading, scoring, and commenting on the proposals. It will take you an hour or two to read each of the state grant proposals, then more time to comment on and score them. The good news is that you usually have a week or two to get your assignment done. As you know, people spend countless hours writing grant proposals. They deserve to have careful, committed, unbiased readers review them—in confidence.

You may also be asked to read grants online. You will be assigned a user name and password to a Web site where you can log on to read and score the proposals assigned to you.

Either way, after reading, scoring, and commenting on your assigned proposals, you will probably be asked to drive to the state department of education offices to meet with the panel of people who have read the same proposals. After an orientation session, you will meet in small groups and discuss the proposals you read and scored. You will be asked to justify your scores, compare them to the other panelists, and listen to the others' perspectives. You will see how your scoring compares with theirs and learn which projects will receive funding and which won't.

These state grant review events can last a half-day, a full day, even two or more days. Your expenses will be paid, and you may even receive an honorarium.

Reviewing Federal Grants

Once you have cut your grant-reading teeth on local and state grant proposals, it may be time to volunteer to read federal grant proposals. Reading federal grant proposals gives you an excellent idea of what is required in submitting one. Several areas in the Department of Education use grant readers. Before you volunteer, check out the Web site or make some calls to see where your interests lie and where your background would make the best fit.

The federal government needs qualified volunteers to read grant proposals for programs like the U.S. Department of Education Office of Postsecondary Education Teacher Quality Enhancement Grant Program. This office is usually seeking new, qualified field reader candidates. When you contact them, they will ask you for a two-page resume and a cover letter requesting inclusion in the Higher Education Field Reader System registry. Information on HEP programs can be found at <http://www.ed.gov/about/offices/list/ope/programs.html>.

Reading federal grant proposals is grueling work and is not a pastime for those with low energy or who prefer a slow pace and lower expectations. Typically, if you are selected to read federal grant proposals, you will be asked to travel to Washington, D.C., where you will meet in a hotel with a large group of proposal readers and alternates. You will be given orientation, be assigned to a team of six to eight readers, and be expected to follow a rigorous schedule of reading, scoring, and discussion.

Federal grant proposals are long and complex, and the scoring rubrics are intricate. Readers must provide written comments for each section, carefully based on the scoring rubrics. The days you spend reading grant proposals are long and lonely; you may find yourself locked in your hotel room reading and writing for days on end. Writer's cramp is an occupational hazard. The pressure is tight to get your daily assignment of grant proposals read, scored, discussed, and approved. It is not uncommon for several new proposal readers to drop out because of stress as the week in Washington progresses. That is why alternates are appointed for each federal grant review project.

When you read federal grant proposals, you will find yourself running with the big dogs. It is worth the effort that you give, however. You will quickly learn what makes a fundable proposal and gain insight into the scope of a federal grant-writing project. Plus, you are being a good citizen when you volunteer to review grant proposals; you are serving as a steward of the taxpayers' dollars.

You begin to see that applying for a federal grant really is within your capabilities. You need a solid idea, a strong proposal writing team, a gung-ho collaborating partner or institution, and some time to work on the proposal. You can do it.

A Grant Proposal Reader's Responsibilities

As a proposal reviewer, you will be expected to:
- Identify any conflict of interest,
- Give specific written feedback for each application,
- Provide helpful written suggestions to the writer,
- Review the grant proposals objectively, without bias or personal feelings,
- Join in the discussion when the review team meets together,
- Keep all information confidential,
- Document your critique and provide a rationale, and
- Use tact and discretion.

In addition, practiced grant proposal readers offer these tips:
- Take notes while reading,
- Read quickly and with purpose,
- Focus on the information related to the scoring rubric,
- Look for key words and phrases, and
- Have a calculator nearby.

Learn from Reading Grant Proposals

You will probably find that your performance as a grant reader, as well as writer, will improve with experience. You will begin to see some of the more common mistakes grant writers make, such as failure to follow directions, unclear writing, and nonspecific or inaccurate budgets.

Another common error you may encounter is the proposal writer's assuming too much prior information on the part of the reader. In their familiarity with their school, its programs, and its community, writers sometimes forget that the proposal reader likely knows nothing about their schools, communities, or students. The reader may be totally unfamiliar with the content of the proposal. As you read and score grant proposals, you will begin to see how some writers have a knack for describing their populations, defining their projects succinctly, and presenting a compelling need for the project.

After performing this proposal-reading service for others, you will gain confidence in your ability to write winning grant proposals. You will also become a more valuable resource to your school community because you will learn what grant money is available and how to access it.

Be sure that your principal and superintendent are aware if you are given the honor of reading grant proposals. When you look good, they look good. It is good for your school and your district when you are selected to review grant proposals. It's an experience you can add to your resume.

Internal Review Team

Some organizations that write and submit grant proposals on a regular basis organize internal review teams. They write the grant proposal well in advance of the submission deadline and then have their own team evaluate their proposal against the proposal guidelines and scoring rubric, revising the proposal to reflect the internal feedback. By the time the grant is submitted, the kinks probably are worked out.

There is nothing to prevent you, your library clerk, and a volunteer or two from performing the same analysis on your proposals. These folks care as much as you do and have everything to gain for their efforts. Be objective. Step back and take an unbiased look. Where do you need more supporting details? Where are you redundant? Where are you understating the case? We will talk more about revising your work later.

Build a Grant-Writing Team

The easiest way for most people to apply for a grant is as a member of a team. Assembling an eager team to help you write your proposal and working together to accomplish your goals can be rewarding. You strengthen your own role as the idea person when you include others' ideas in your proposal. More participants may also broaden your project's appeal to your potential grantor.

Cooperative learning, an effective strategy in the classroom, is equally effective in grant-seeking. Having assigned roles makes the task easier and the process smoother for all.

As you assemble a grant writing team, consider including some variation of the following roles. You may find yourself and your colleagues playing more than one role. Consider seeking potential team members on a library listserv, among friends and colleagues at neighboring schools or library school, or family members.

- *Reader*

  The person in this critical position reads the request for proposal (RFP) carefully, highlighting vital information such as the date the proposal is due, maximum length, type size, font, and spacing required. The reader could be you, your spouse, your school secretary, a library aide, or a clerk.

- *Abstract Writer*

  This person can see the big picture of your grant proposal and describe it accurately and compactly in one powerful page. Write the abstract yourself, if succinct, expository writing is your forte. If not, get a friend, a colleague, or your boss to write this one-page summary of your project.

- *Number Cruncher*

  You will need an accountant-type person on your team to calculate the budget you'll need, adjust it as you revise your proposal, and check that it meets all the criteria specified in the RFP. You will need a budget narrative, a written description of the budget, and a detailed budget-at-a-glance. Each reference to costs in your proposal needs to match budget figures. The budget needs to include nitty-gritty details—when stipends are paid, cost of salaries, Federal Insurance Contributions Act (FICA) deductions, and other benefits.

- *Researcher*

  You will probably be required to cite research that supports your project. The researcher will search the Internet and databases for research that supports your proposal. Literature searches can be time-consuming but worth your time when your findings persuade the grantor to fund your project. This person will need access to school-level data and an ability to interpret the data accurately.

- *Statistician*

  Many organizations make grants only to entities that meet certain race, gender, ethnic, and socioeconomic criteria. The statistician needs to have the perseverance to dig through the archives, ferret out the data required by the RFP, confirm their accuracy, and make sure that you have translated the data correctly to the grant proposal. Treasure these statistics, file them in a safe place, and update them as you receive new information each year. Almost every grant you may apply for will require you to furnish this information.

- *Shopper*
The shopper must be willing to research costs, brands, consultants, and other factors that will impact the source and cost of items and services for which you are requesting funding. What kind of laptop computer mobile labs and related accessories are available and at what cost? Do you need a consultant? What will the consultant cost per day? The success of your application will depend in part on the accuracy of this information. If the grant you seek is for a laptop lab for your library and you underestimate the cost, you are not likely to get the grant.

- *Proofreader*
This person needs to be a whiz at spotting a misused or misspelled word or a grammatical error. She must read and reread the grant proposal from the title page to the last appendix to make sure it is grammatically and syntactically correct. Who proofreads your school newsletter or staff bulletin? Could he help you? Were you an English teacher in a past life? You may have the necessary credentials. You may feel irritated when the proofreader finds a juicy error but treat her kindly, for you need her.

- *Veteran*
Every proposal-writing team needs a veteran who has written successful proposals. This guru will give you tips as you write and keep you motivated with tales of treasure at the end of the grant-proposal rainbow. Your principal, library coordinator, or next-door teacher may fill the bill. Educators are usually eager to assist one another.

- *Editor*
Someone needs to assemble the component sections into one coherent document. Look for a person who is a whiz at word processing and a master of consistent, coherent writing. The editor makes the team-written proposal speak with one voice; ensures that headings, type faces and sizes, and other format considerations conform to the RFP stipulations; and that headings match the wording in the table of contents.

Has the superintendent of schools signed in the required spot? Are the attachments secured to the document or are they still in a stack of papers beside your computer? The editor looks after these details while putting the final grant proposal together.

- *Key Communicator*

  This person's job is to keep the boss in the loop. He reports to the central office intermittently to ensure that the proposal is in sync with school board policy, state purchasing guidelines, and the like and makes sure that all staff members potentially affected by the grant understand their roles and are amenable to the plan.

- *Delivery Person*

  Somebody has to make sure the precious cargo of your grant proposal gets where it is going. The fine print in the RFP will tell you how and where the document must be delivered. This responsible citizen makes sure the grant proposal is delivered on time in the proper container to the right recipient.

- *Copy Maker*

  Everyone who participated in writing the proposal, as well as those who will have a role in the project if it is funded, will need a copy of the final product. The business office will also need a copy if you will be making purchases through the school district's purchasing department. Your boss needs a copy and you need a copy for your file. If the document is on the hard-drive of your computer, be sure you have a clean copy on CD and memory stick or USB drive, too.

- *Pace Keeper*

  Completing your proposal means keeping on schedule. Once you know the due date for the grant proposal, you can work backwards to establish interim due dates. Weekly meetings keep your team motivated without overwhelming them, though you may need to meet daily as you near completion.

Rarely will you have the luxury to have this many people on your grant-writing team. You'll probably have to wear several of the hats yourself. The hours for grant writers are long and pay is poor, so serve coffee and maybe even food at your meetings. Make sure that your own company is good. As U.S. anthropologist Margaret Mead (1901 – 1978) said, "Never doubt that a small group of thoughtful, committed citizens can change the world. Indeed, it is the only thing that ever has."

Find out if your school district has a grant proposal writer on staff. Many do, some full-time, others in addition to other duties. If you are fortunate to have such a person in your district, call and make an appointment to see her. Show her your plan and ask for her help. If she cannot help you with the actual writing, she may give you feedback and coach you as you write the proposal. There is usually someone who can help with the budget, at least.

Meet with Your Team

Once you have formed a team, schedule a planning meeting. You have several tasks to do and many questions to answer. You will want to:

- Establish the goals of your project,
- Define a timeline,
- Refine the goals of the grant writing team positions,
- Schedule your next meeting, and
- Set group norms.

Prior to the meeting, make enough copies of the RFP or grant application guidelines so that each person can have one. Highlight the sections of the application that give pertinent specifications, instructions, and pointers for sections. More specific suggestions for highlighting will be given later.

Brainstorm an outline for your project. If you've already established the parameters and design of your project, see how they fit with the proposal specifications.

Decide which partnerships and alliances, if any, you want to establish for the project—perhaps collaborate with another school library in your district, in another school district, or even in a private school. You may want to team with a state entity, a public library, or a private company such as a software vendor. Collaborating with community entities is often a huge plus to funders.

As a team, decide who will do which tasks:

- Set your meeting schedules,
- Organize the agendas for the meetings,
- Establish internal deadlines, and
- Agree on document format.

The whole is greater than the sum of its parts. Your grant proposal has a much higher probability of success when you write it with a gung-ho team of experts.

Let's review the tasks you may wish to assign yourself at this point in your project:

- Research ways to become a grant proposal reader,
- Volunteer to be a contest judge,
- Explore education and other local foundations,
- Volunteer to read state and/or federal grant proposals,
- Begin to form a grant writing team, and
- Meet with the team to set goals and establish a schedule for your project.

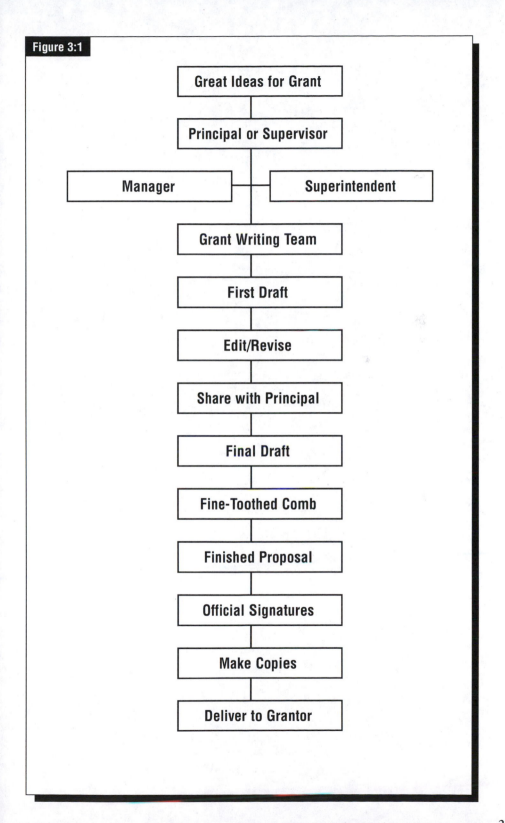

Figure 3:1

Great Ideas for Grant

Principal or Supervisor

Manager | Superintendent

Grant Writing Team

First Draft

Edit/Revise

Share with Principal

Final Draft

Fine-Toothed Comb

Finished Proposal

Official Signatures

Make Copies

Deliver to Grantor

Chapter 4

Read the Fine Print

In the long run, men hit only what they aim at.

— Henry David Thoreau

Read the Application

It is easy to develop the bad habit of reading the directions only when all else fails. This habit and the act of writing a successful grant are at complete odds. It is absolutely critical in grant-seeking to scrutinize the entire application.

First Reading

Make yourself a copy of the RFP and sit down with it and a highlighter pen. Each time you see a specific direction, highlight it. Some examples are:

- Date the grant is due,
- Size of print and type of font,
- Formatting rules,
- Spacing requirements,
- Maximum length of abstract, sections, entire document, and whether appendices are allowed/required,
- Required attachments,
- Budget restrictions,

- Required signatures,
- Points possible for each section,
- Funding priorities,
- Mailing address or URL for electronic submission,
- Number of copies to submit,
- Application deadline,
- Special requirements or restrictions, including:
    Collaboration,
    Letters of commitment or support,
    Whether appendices are allowed,
    Statistical data, and
    Resumes.

When you have thoroughly highlighted each section of the proposal, begin reading it again. It takes several reads before the gist of a complicated proposal request becomes clear. There are so many details and directions that one reading may turn you away from grant writing forever. Stick with it.

Second and Third Readings

On your second reading, watch for and highlight in a second color any buzzwords the prospective grantor seems to like so that you have your important instructions in one color and colorful language in another. If the grantor wants proposals to serve the "have-nots in the digital divide," highlight that phrase and plan to include it in your proposal. Highlight any powerful or distinctive words or phrases your target audience seems to favor, and be sure to employ them in your proposal.

Pay close attention to the points each of the sections is worth. Obviously, you will want to spend your greatest energy where you can score the most points.

Read carefully to learn how your project fits the donor's priorities. Find out what the philanthropy will and will not fund. Read between the lines for hints that will help you recognize what might persuade this organization to underwrite your program.

Reading the fine print is a key step in writing a winning grant. On your third reading, use a third color of highlighter to mark any examples of successful proposals that the grantor has included.

Make Copies

Once you have highlighted the nitty-gritty directions and power language, make color copies for your grant writing team. If you do not have access to a color printer, make copies and highlight each copy. While this may seem like a time-consuming effort, you will be thankful later. You are really learning the donor's rules and regulations as you read and reread the application. Your writer's eye is learning more about this person or organization each time you read the application.

The more you understand this benefactor's priorities, the more likely it is you will write a winning grant proposal. The grantor will not change funding priorities because you have written an excellent proposal if your project is outside his priorities. He is looking for a perfect match. Read to learn what his priorities are and how you can make them yours.

One thing you may learn from reading the RFP is that the application deadline is so close that you do not have time to put an appropriate proposal together. If that is the case, don't despair. If this grant is an annual event, you and your team may decide that you want to begin work now on a proposal to submit next year.

Getting Ready to Write

As you prepare to write a draft of your grant proposal you will need to stock up on:
- Paper,
- Pencils,
- Pens,
- Highlighters,
- Grammar reference book,
- Thesaurus,
- Dictionary, and
- Style manual.

Make sure you have access to a computer, printer, and photocopier.

Even before meeting with your grant-writing team, you can start a document on your computer. Identify and label each section of the proposal and the subheadings under them. Type in "Date due" and "Team member" under each heading. Then when you meet with your grant-writing team, you can agree on the interim due dates and pencil them in on the copies of the document sections you have typed and copied for the team meetings. As team members volunteer to contribute to a section, you will pencil their names in at your team meeting.

If there are subheadings within sections, type those in your document outline.

Abstract

Date due _____

Team member _____

(1 page)

(Include project needs, goals, plan, budget amount, evaluation)

Save as You Go

Save your grant proposal on a CD or memory stick as you work and again when it is complete. That way you can edit, revise, rewrite, and resubmit it for future competitions. You will find that a proposal can be resubmitted several times to different donors with just a little revision. If you do resubmit a proposal with revisions, be meticulously careful to change all pertinent information. Readers are turned off by careless references to another proposal.

Call for Clarification

Don't be afraid to call or e-mail the grantor. Now is the time to call the program officer if there is something in the RFP that you do not understand or something for which you need clarification. When you call, you may also learn recent information that was not included in the RFP.

Be ready to take notes. Listen carefully and use your best telephone manners. When you briefly describe your project, does it sound like it fits with the priorities of the sponsor? Make a list of your questions before you call so you don't waste a minute of the officer's time.

- How much money will be spent on the new projects they will be funding?
- How many applications for that money do they anticipate?
- What common errors do applicants make?
- Are their grants ever renewable?
- What would they like to see in a proposal?
- Do they ever review drafts of a proposal and give feedback before the proposal is formally submitted?
- Can they give you a copy of a previously funded proposal that you could read?
- Is it possible for you to have a copy of the reviewer's scoring form?
- Will the organization be offering an RFP workshop? If so, where and when will that be?

If there is a workshop, attend. You can collaborate with others seeking the same funds, meet the sponsor and learn more about the competition. Don't miss an opportunity like this.

Assess Your Proposal

Ask someone outside of your field to read your proposal. Do you have a sibling who is not in education who would be willing to evaluate it? Find a sharp-eyed but kind reader who is not a school librarian. Give him a copy of your proposal and ask him to note any questions or comments he has. If he can't tell you in just a few words what your proposal's mission is, how it will be accomplished, and why it is significant, then you clearly can't expect to win a grant. It is time to revise and rewrite to strengthen and clarify your proposal.

Read Some Winning Grant Proposals before you put the cursor to the screen to write your own. You wouldn't expect to perform a swan dive on your first try without first watching many good examples. Don't expect to win a grant without reading several winning entries first.

Winning grant proposals are available for reading on the Internet and on the accompanying CD. You will find some at the U.S. Department of Education Web site, <http://www.ed.gov>. Just as you would not want to score student writing before reading samples scored by experts, don't try to write a grant proposal without first reading several winning examples.

Proposal Letter

Some donors prefer to receive a proposal letter before or in place of a formal proposal. A proposal letter is a short grant proposal, usually two to four pages long, written in letter form. The letter explains what you intend to accomplish in a concise and compelling manner. A proposal letter is sometimes called a concept paper. With some private donors, a compelling letter proposal is all that is needed to secure a grant. Others use the proposal letter as a way to screen prospective grantees.

Multiple Submissions

Some grant-seekers prefer to submit their proposals to several funding sources at the same time. If you choose to make multiple submissions, be sure that you let each recipient know you are submitting the proposal to other funding sources. There are pros and cons to multiple submissions. The pros are that your eggs are not in one basket and you are casting your potential funding net in a broad area.

A con of making multiple submissions would be that you are using a shotgun versus a rifle approach. Can you find a benefactor whose mission is a perfect match to yours? If so, aim at that one target. If not, consider shopping your proposal around.

If you wait for perfect conditions, you will never get anything done. Keep that thought in mind and get started on your project. Where are you on your "to do" list? Have you:

- Read the application several times?
- Made copies and highlighted critical information?
- Gathered the necessary office supplies and equipment?
- Started a draft document on your computer?
- Called the program officer?
- Found another reader to evaluate your proposal?
- Read several examples of funded grant proposals?
- Written a proposal letter?

If so, you are well on your way to success.

Chapter 5

Parts of the Proposal

Writing is the hardest way of earning a living, with the possible exception of wrestling alligators.

— Olin Miller

Proposal Components

In order to take some of the mystery out of writing a grant proposal, let's define the parts of the proposal. Note that the application or RFP for competitive grant proposals usually states the number of points possible for each section. It is critical for you to match your effort in the development of each of the grant sections to the number of points you can gain.

As a rule of thumb, if there is a page limit to your finished proposal—and there usually is—you should allot yourself a number of pages for each section proportionate to the percentage of points for that section. If the proposal is limited to 10 pages and 100 points are possible, then you can figure you should allot three pages to the Plan of Action if it is worth 30 points.

For your proposal to stand out from the rest, it needs to offer a distinctive and innovative solution for a defined problem, written in a compelling manner.

Cover Letter

Sometimes you are allowed a cover letter for your proposal, sometimes not. If you do include a cover letter, make sure it presents a clear picture of the problem, the proposed solution, and the anticipated outcomes. It should be one or two pages long, no longer. As you describe the project, tell the reader the anticipated cost and the expected results without repeating all the information in the formal proposal. The cover letter should set the stage and make the reader want to get to the actual proposal.

Your letter should be concise and well written. It should include a synopsis of your budget and briefly introduce the personnel involved. Tell how your proposal will further the grantor's mission and give the reviewer an incentive to read your proposal carefully. The best plan is to write the cover letter last and make it persuasive. View it as the appetizer to a full-course dinner.

Title Page

The title page features the project title and the name of the applicant organization. The grant guidelines will give specific directions regarding what can and cannot be on the title page. Follow them carefully. Writing the title page first can give you a great sense of accomplishment; now you have one section down, just a few more to write.

Unless the RFP directs otherwise, provide your project title, your library's name, and the name of the funding source to which you are applying on the title page. Center this information about one-third of the way down the page. In the lower right-hand corner include your name, address, phone number, and the date. If you are applying for funds for your school library, include the name of your school, the school address and phone number, e-mail address, URL, and the name of your school district.

Figure 5:1

Gather Round
A Storytelling Workshop Proposal

Blue Skies School Library
Application to Gotrocks Foundation

Ima Goodlibrarian
1234 Storybook Lane
888.987.6543
Ima@blueskies.k12.org
Date

Table of Contents

If your proposal is five or more pages long and the application allows it, include a table of contents. The table of contents page should follow the title page and list the page numbers of the major sections and all of the appendices.

Abstract, Project Summary, or Executive Summary

Sometimes this section is called the **executive summary**. Like a newspaper lead, it includes the **who**, **what**, **where, when,** and **why** of your project. The abstract is a brief, clear, and concise summary of your proposed project. It is a one-page snapshot of how much money you need, what you want it for, and how it will improve the achievement and the lives of your students—in about 250 words. The abstract section must be short, powerful, and cause the reader to want to read on. What is the problem and how are you going to solve it?

As a challenge, see if you can summarize your whole proposal in one sentence that says who you are, your claim to fame, what you want the grantor to do for you, your budget request, and the major benefits your project will have. Include your project title in the abstract or project summary. If you are successful, your benefactor may use this section for public relations purposes.

If space permits, include background information about your community, your school, and student achievement data. If you have special credentials that make you well qualified to manage this project, include them—awards you have won, outstanding accomplishments, previous grant proposals, or other evidence of your unique qualifications to manage this project. If there is not space in this section, your credentials will fit well in the personnel section.

The grantor does not want to hear how our jobs will be made easier but instead how the lives and skills of students will improve. The grantor wants to know what about your proposal fits perfectly with his mission.

Statement of Need

This section states the problem: what needs to be fixed or improved in your program, library, or school. Focus on the needs of others–students, teachers, parents, local community. Use data to paint a picture of the situation you hope to improve, cite research that supports the need and the proposed solution, and then tie your program back to school, district, state, and national achievement goals.

Keep the sponsor's values in mind as you describe your needs. How can funding your project help the sponsor meet its institutional goals? How can you convince the funding agency that your effort and expertise coupled with a specific process, technique, program, or curricular change will remove a barrier or solve the problem you are highlighting?

If you have performed some type of needs assessment that led you to make a long-range plan and seek grant funds, include a summary of that data in your statement of needs. Powerful data, presented well, will make your case convincing. Use student achievement data whenever possible.

Most grants require demographic data. Find statistics from your school, district, and community that support your claim of need for the project you propose. Tell your potential benefactor why this project is necessary. Again, tie your project to your school, state, and national goals.

Cite relevant statistics to help you make your case. Use graphs, but don't overload the reader with too many or irrelevant statistics. Find support in the literature for the project you are proposing. Search your topic on the Internet for more sources. Are there national or local task force reports that support your plan?

Use comments from local newspaper articles or comments from teachers or students that support the perceived need for your project. Beware of using phrases like "little is known about . . .," "no research has been done on . . . ," or "there is no information about . . . ." Do your best to find some evidence to support the need for your particular plan.

> *The successful proposal will focus on others, not on self.*

Make your needs statement specific, not so broad and general that you are describing the woes of the world in general. If you are asking for backpacks for students to carry home library books so their parents can read aloud to them, outline your school's reading comprehension scores. Find journals or published research articles that support the merit of reading aloud to children.

Do not present the case that your students need a laptop computer lab. The case you want to present is that your students need to acquire information retrieval and evaluation skills. They need to improve communication skills. Those are the needs that are causing you to seek a computer lab and the appropriate online databases for them. If you find yourself presenting a case for needing "things," you have not yet refined your needs far enough. State your needs in terms of student outcomes, not equipment.

While your needs statement must be factual and include evidence, try also to put a genuine emotional spin on it. Cite an example of a real life situation that will be improved if your project is funded. If your students' needs are urgent, work that into your statement. Be sure your benefactor is clear on why your project will be a good investment.

It's a rare grantor who is interested in your personal needs or comfort. Even though your project may improve your working conditions or efficiency, that would not be a compelling argument for the grant. The successful proposal will focus on others, not on self.

Goals and Objectives

In this section of your proposal, explain how your project will address the needs that you described in the previous section. List the goals and objectives that will be accomplished if your project is funded. Focus on academic values.

The goals should clearly state the end result of the project. Goals are an aim or a purpose. You will want a maximum of two or three goals for your project, no more. Do not try to do too much in one grant. Writing measurable goals initially that link directly to the evaluation component of the project is a wise endeavor. Keep the goals simple and measurable, and tie them directly to the evaluation. Keep in mind the assessments that are already routinely given in your school. See if you can tag on to those to measure and evaluate the goals of your project.

Describe which population, such as students or teachers, will receive what services. State the goals in terms of staff and student needs, not your own. A goal should be a sentence, not a paragraph. The project goals should be concise and overarching. Consider listing your goals in order of importance.

Objectives explain what is going to be done and when and how it is going to be done. Not all grants ask for both goals and objectives to be identified. If the grant does require it, the donor will want to know how students, teachers, or parents will acquire or refine which skills. Make objectives measurable and specific and include strategies. Objectives must be directly related to the evaluation of your project, and they must be measurable. For example: By May 2013, 85 percent of the students in the school district in grade three will score as proficient or higher on state reading proficiency tests.

Don't confuse your objectives with your methods or your action plan. The objectives are the ends and methods are the means. Goals are the long-range, broad statements of your vision. The objectives are the short, specific, measurable plans to achieve the long-range goals. The objectives will provide solutions to the needs outlined earlier in your proposal. The objectives should be reasonable and achievable. Do not forget that it is critical to align your project's goals and objectives with the grantor's.

Clearly hook your goals and objectives to your school or library's mission statement. Be positive in your writing; be sure to mention if your project is addressing a need not being addressed by any other project.

Your project will probably begin with a set of objectives and end with the accomplishment of these broad goals. What will be the benchmarks of your program's success? Your objectives state what you intend to change and what benchmarks you plan to use to demonstrate success. Your objectives are tied directly to the evaluation of your program.

Plan of Action

Now is the time to let your inner journalist take over. **What** are you planning to do? **Who** will be providing services to whom? **How** much will it cost and how will the money be spent? **When** and **where** will this happen?

The plan of action is a capsule summary of how the planned project will be implemented. Sometimes this section is called the **project description**.

This section tells the details of how you will achieve your goals. In your final draft, you must be organized, sequential, and succinct. Describe your planned actions on a specific timeline. If staff are being trained, include the training schedule. Specify clearly what you plan to do.

Your plan of action must be engaging and innovative to be funded. In today's educational climate, your plan should include problem-based learning and your students should be deeply engaged in it. In order to appeal to benefactors and to be current, your activities could address:

- Reading, math, and science,
- Research-based instructional strategies,
- Innovative curriculum to improve student achievement,
- Staff development plans,
- Parental involvement programs and events,
- Collaborations with staff and with other entities,
- National, state, and local standards,
- Academic achievement,
- Authentic assessment,
- Multiple learning modalities, and
- Family literacy.

Curb Appeal and Focus on Students

Make it look good; it will pay. In your plan, make your use of technology fresh and innovative and be sure that it is well integrated in the learning process. Keep the focus on the students and the impact that the project will have on them. Whenever possible, include staff development in your plan.

Consider describing:

- Where your project will take place,
- Instructional strategies you will use,
- Participants in the project,
- Personnel conducting or managing the project,
- Stages and phases of the project, and
- A timeline of events.

It might be helpful to list the activities with a timeline or on a chart so that you can describe your plan in chronological order. Computer software can make chart-making a breeze.

Budget

This section includes a financial description of your project with explanatory notes. One page will be the budget sheet, and the other will be the budget narrative. Most RFPs include a specific form sheet upon which to record your budget plans. In addition to the budget sheet, there is usually a budget narrative in which you must accurately state what funds you will need and how you are planning to spend them. You must be sure that these two match at all stages.

What will be the financial requirements for your project? The grantor will want to see realistic figures and a realistic timeline for making expenditures. The grantor will also want to know how you are going to keep track of funds and record progress–that you are fiscally responsible.

Phases. If your project will occur in phases, be sure to note the estimated costs associated with each phase. Make sure the grantor understands why you need the outside funding. Try to anticipate questions like, "Why can't you use your school district funds for these items?"

In-Kind. Some RFPs require a list of in-kind budget items your institution will provide. This request refers to the services or supplies that will be provided by you, your media center, your school, or your district. An example of an in-kind service would be donating your time and talent to conducting an evening workshop for parents to help them learn to read aloud to their children. If you would not be paid for the workshop, your services would be an in-kind contribution to the project. Parents volunteering their time would be another example. In-kind contributions can be considered a method of cost-sharing.

Cost-Sharing and Indirect Costs. Cost-sharing is usually the amount of the project that is not funded by the donor. It often includes donated effort, or in-kind contributions, but it rarely includes funds from the grantee. Indirect costs are expenses that are shared or incurred for common objectives between the grantor and the grantee and cannot be easily or specifically connected with one activity. They include things like rent, or support from information technology staff, the business office, and others.

Categories. Organize your budget expenses into major categories:
- Materials or supplies,
- Equipment,
- Salaries,
- Employee benefits and FICA payments,

- Travel,
- Consultants, professional services and contracts,
- Personnel,
- Communications, and
- Publicity and publications.

Estimate Accurately. Do not underestimate your budget needs. If you do, the grantor may think you have not done your homework. Be realistic; plan for the unexpected. Do careful research. Make phone calls, get online, print out price lists, and order catalogs. Once you have these figures, you can better estimate your total budget needs.

Extra effort and attention will help you avoid underestimating your needs. The granting organization may question your competence in other areas if you cannot accurately predict the financial needs of your project. Then later, if you do get your grant, you may be in trouble when you try to implement the program with inadequate funding. How will you complete your project? Now is the time for you to carefully think through the costs of your project, bearing in mind that it may take as long as a year before you begin to receive funding and costs may have increased by then. Remember that there are unanticipated costs even in the best-laid plans.

Make It Look Good. Use a spreadsheet format with an appropriate title. Round off your figures to the nearest $10, $50, or $100. Set your spreadsheet program to align the figures and provide subtotals within each section. Consider using a money management software program to help you develop your budget. Give your proposal curb appeal.

Salaries. Be cautious about budgeting salaries of new employees in your proposal. Once the grant has ended, who will fund those positions? Most school district leaders are leery of seeking grants that commit the school district to funding new staff positions in the future. If you need personnel help, can you pay stipends to employees already on the payroll? Can you contract with a consultant for services so you will not be obligated for future expenses once the services have been performed?

Many grant proposal writers suggest that you avoid requesting funds for hiring staff when you can. Usually, your school district will not be interested in adding positions.

Other Costs. Do not forget to include postage, office supplies, printing, and the like. Make sure your budget contains no unexplained amounts. Keep records of how you arrived at your budget figures. You will need them if budget modifications are required or if your budget is questioned.

Make Changes Carefully. Be careful as you progress in writing your proposal. When you make changes in your proposal, remember to make corresponding changes in your budget. It is easy to change parts of the proposal and forget to change the budget section. Few things can turn a grantor off faster than a budget that does not match the proposal.

Multiple Funding Sources. If you plan to have multiple funding sources, note that in your budget. Be careful to describe funds from other entities that you have already secured for your project. Include a timeline in your budget. When will your other funds arrive and for how long a time period will they be available?

Be Honest. Be financially honest; do your budget homework carefully. Include legitimate in-kind services and genuine funding from other sources. Where else have you asked for grant funds for this very project? Be fair. Don't shortchange yourself, but don't even think of padding the budget.

Use the Generic. In normal circumstances, you will write your budget using generic terms, not brand names. Although you may want to specify the platform of your computer, Windows® or Mac®, you will probably want to write your budget using generic terms such as " laptop computer" or "MP3 players."

Cautions. Requesting funds to pay stipends for teachers or consultants is reasonable. Do not forget to include funds for benefits such as health care and Social Security. Detail those fringe benefits separately from salaries.

Without specific permission from the superintendent and school board, do not obligate your school or school district to spend money in order to accept a grant. Beware of the phrase, "matching funds." Do not apply for anything requiring matching funds from your school system without the permission of the powers-that-be.

Mention major budget expenditures within the body of your proposal so that the budget section makes good sense to the reader. See the CD for samples.

Be aware that you may need to adjust your budget later. It is not uncommon for a proposal to be considered for funding provided that the budget is modified according to the donor's specifications. Be open to new ideas and ways of executing your project, if the need arises.

Personnel

The benefactors want to know who are the key players in your grant proposal. In the personnel section you will provide a brief description of your staff—number of full-time paid staff members, part-time staff members, and volunteers. Include only information relevant to this project.

Credentials, Job Descriptions, Resumes, and Biographical Sketches. You will ordinarily write a paragraph describing the credentials and special skills of each of the participants in the grant. You may need to include resumes or curricula vitae of all the participants. Summarize your school's or your district's expertise and show how it supports your proposal.

If, for instance, your principal, the head librarian at the local community college, and you are writing this grant together, those are the people you will highlight in the personnel section, listing all their pertinent degrees, certifications, honors, and awards.

One of your objectives in this section is to establish your credentials and demonstrate why you are capable of accomplishing this project. Make sure the grantor understands that you are a member of a viable organization (your school), that you have a good solid idea, and that you are a capable project manager. Tell why you are uniquely qualified to solve the problem for which your project is designed. The benefactor wants to know your track record. If you have received other grants, list them. This is a powerful indicator in the eyes of the funder that you can handle the project.

Job Descriptions. Include job descriptions if the RFP or application contains those requirements.

Resumes. If you are applying for and implementing the grant yourself, include your resume. (See sample resumes on the CD.) There are many other excellent resume samples and helpful sites on the Internet; CareerBuilder.com is one.

You may want to save more than one version of your resume in your database. Some of your credentials will be more relevant to one project than to another. Tailor a version of your resume for the intended project.

Do not forget to include examples of your leadership and management skills—serving as PTA president or church stewardship campaign chairman, for instance—but do not list every committee you ever served on or every continuing education class you ever took. Strive for balance.

Keep your resume to one page. Assume your reader is a busy person. If your project is larger, you will probably need to include the resumes of other grant project participants in the appendix.

Biographical Sketches. Some applications ask for biographical sketches instead of resumes. A biographical sketch includes the same information as a resume but is written in third-person narrative form. Think about an author profile on a book jacket. That image will help you get started writing about yourself in third person. Keep it short (one page or less), focus on your career, and include only the most significant and pertinent information.

Evaluation

You need a method of evaluating the results of your project. This section of your proposal is critical to your success. Experts say that more points are lost here than in almost any other section, so proceed with caution. Conversely, a good evaluation plan will help you win your grant. Clear, understandable evaluation findings will help build support for your program from your administration, your district, and your community. They will increase the sustainability of your project.

Formative or Summative. There are two ways to evaluate a project's effectiveness: either analyze the process that you have put into place or measure some type of product. A process evaluation is a *formative evaluation.* A product evaluation is a *summative evaluation.*

The evaluation process you choose can be critical to your success. Tie it to your objectives. Keep the process simple and manageable while making it meaningful. Ask yourself:

- Will the project impact student test scores?
- What tests or measurements do your students already take that could be used to measure the effect of the grant project?
- What products or results will the proposed project yield?
- How could they be used to evaluate the project's impact?
- Can you display the data on charts or graphs as evaluation data?

Using test data that your school already harvests is a low-cost, effective project evaluation tool. You could also use performance-based assessment or portfolios. What process will you be implementing with the grant project that could be evaluated? Sorry, anecdotal information is no longer considered meaningful in program evaluations. Smiles on their precious faces are nice, but do not use this as the sole evidence of the effectiveness of your project.

- Would your circulation statistics serve as an evaluation measurement?
- Will your library circulation figures increase as a result of the grant project?
- Will the reading teacher need to give an informal reading inventory to the students before and after your project?
- Is she willing to do that and does your principal support that assessment?
- Do you need special permission from parents to test? Do you need to budget for the cost of the tests and their administration?

Other ways of collecting data are interviews, observations by staff or experts, and examination of records.

Evaluating Technology. If your proposal is for some type of educational technology, remember that technology is a means-to-an-end learning. Technology is not an end unto itself. If you are asking for technology for students, be prepared to show what increase in student achievement can be expected and how you will measure it. If you are requesting high-tech equipment, make sure your plan is student-centered. What data will you use to demonstrate that your students have progressed academically as a result of your project?

- Will they be able to make better grades, score higher on tests or other assessments, complete more challenging coursework, or demonstrate mastery of skills?
- Will they stay in school longer?
- Will you reduce the drop-out rate? How can you measure that?
- Does the technology make learning easier? If so, how can you measure it?
- What overall impact will the project have on student achievement and how can that be measured?

Test Resources. If you want to use test data and need more information about existing evaluation instruments, take a look at Buros' *Mental Measurements Yearbook* (University of Nebraska Press). This lists tests in many fields and describes each test. The Buros Web site is <www.unl.edu/buros>. Another resource for testing instruments is the *ETS Collection Catalog*, published by the Educational Testing Service <www.ets.org>.

Evaluation Methods. The grantor wants to know that the grant dollars will be well spent. You will typically need to provide evidence of the impact of the grant on your population at the end of the grant period. Try to keep the measurement of impact as simple as possible. Following are some evaluation methods to consider:
- Test scores,
- Circulation,
- Number of visits to the library,
- Traffic on your Web site,
- Staff development,
- Parent, staff, or student surveys, and
- Attendance and drop-out rates

Interim Reports. You may be asked to provide both interim and final reports describing your project. These reports may fulfill a type of evaluation requirement. A typical report would include budget expenditures, attendance or enrollment records of project participants, summaries of accomplishments, and other data. Consider submitting an interim report whether you are required to or not.

Evaluation Consultation. If you do not feel confident writing the evaluation section of your proposal, consider contacting a colleague in higher education to ask for assistance or guidance. One of the keys to designing an evaluation section is to make sure you have meaningful and measurable objectives. That will make writing your evaluation component much easier.

Review Other Evaluation Components. Another source of help is the evaluation section of successful grant proposals. The best evaluation plans are specific and meaningful, not vague and unfocused. If there will be a cost associated with your evaluation component, include it in your budget. Keep it simple. The grantor wants to know if the project worked.

- Identify what will be evaluated,
- Decide the method of evaluation to use,
- Employ the method, and
- Analyze and summarize the data.

Timeline

Many RFPs ask for a detailed timeline; usually, the larger the grant, the longer the project takes to complete. While a $500 grant may have a very simple timeline, a $200,000 grant will require a more elaborate one. The $500 grant project may take a semester, while the $200,000 one may span two or three school years.

Dissemination

Most RFPs today ask the grantee to delineate a plan by which the project and its results can be shared with a wider audience, thus multiplying its value. Some dissemination strategies are:

- Project newsletter,
- Workshops designed to share the project,
- Site visits,
- Interim and final reports on the progress of the project,
- Presentations at local, state, regional, national, and international conferences,
- Journal articles,
- Informative brochures,
- Podcasts,
- Library Web page,
- Demonstrations of methods and materials, and
- Press conferences.

The dissemination section of your proposal should identify:
A timeline for dissemination activities,

- Personnel responsible for dissemination,
- Budget for dissemination activities,
- Target audience for the dissemination information,
- Methods for distributing printed and virtual materials, and
- Methods for evaluating the dissemination activities.

Sustainability

Some grant applications require you to describe the sustainability of your proposed project. Even if there is no specific section for this, it is best to cover this topic somewhere in your proposal. The benefactor wants to know that once the seed money is gone and you have cashed the final grant check, your organization can sustain the project. Once the grant is completed, will you need additional funding or can your regular budget support the project?

Letters of Support

Many applications request that you submit letters of support. If you are collaborating with another local entity, the funding organization wants evidence of support from upper management of both organizations. They want to know if your principal, your superintendent, and your parent organization supports your effort. Letters of support may be required from any of the following:

- The superintendent of schools,
- The college president,
- The dean,
- The chief operating officer,
- The chief financial officer,
- The head librarian,
- The director of curriculum and instruction,
- The chairperson of the school site council,
- The president of the PTA or PTO,
- The president of the teachers' association,
- Your city's mayor, or
- Someone from the state department of education who is familiar with your accomplishments as they relate to this project.

Not all letters of support are created equal. You be the judge, but consider not including letters that are so generic and nonspecific that they lend no weight to your cause. Do include letters that are well written, compelling, and likely to increase your chances of success. See some samples on the CD.

Certification and Signatures

Many grant applications require a form certifying your nonprofit or tax-exempt status. Your school system's business office can help you with IRS Form 501(c)3 and other documentation to meet this requirement.

Many applications require the signature of the head of your organization—usually the superintendent of schools. Plan far ahead to get the necessary signatures.

Attachments, Supporting Documentation, and Appendices

Some RFPs will specify types of attachments you may include with your proposal. A brochure about your library, one describing your school, and a third describing your district might be appropriate. If you don't already have these brochures, don't feel you need to produce them for the project.

If there is a recent news article about your school and it is relevant to your project, include it. Other attachments might be:

- Organizational charts,
- Fiscal reports or budgets,
- Agency publications,
- Award descriptions,
- Diagrams or schematics of proposed equipment requests, and
- Your school's report card or annual report, if your state issues them.

Attach only carefully selected items that directly support your proposal and nothing unless the RFP specifically requests it. Do not make more work for your proposal reader. Highlight pertinent sections of journal or newspaper articles to make them easier to read. Most grant application readers do not have time to watch that video you want to send; in fact, an unsolicited video or CD can be irritating. If in doubt about a possible attachment, consult the guidelines in the RFP. Check to make sure you have included everything the granting organization requests and send it in the requested format.

Tip: Set Interim Due Dates

Even if you are working on your own without a grant-writing team, you still need interim due dates. Keep yourself motivated by setting short-term goals. Reward yourself with a latte or some token pleasure when you meet your short-terms goals. You must keep yourself motivated to conquer this beast.

Sample Grant Proposals

There are many examples on the Internet of successful grant proposals. Log on to one of the Web sites, such as Scholastic.com teachers' site, and read some of the proposals. You can find the Scholastic examples at <http://teacher.scholastic.com/professional/grants/sampropo.htm>. See many others on the accompanying CD. Reading proposals that have been funded is an excellent way to learn your way around the sections of a grant proposal.

Chapter 6

Speak Clearly

Your manuscript is both good and original,
but the part that is good is not original
and the part that is original is not good.

—Samuel Johnson

Be Precise and Concise

If you mean *school principal*, say *school principal*, do not say *head learner*. Define your terms. You have a clear understanding of what brain-based education, authentic assessment, and curriculum-based-measurement mean, but do not assume the grant proposal reader does. Educational grant application reading teams almost always include members from business and government, not just educators. A good rule of thumb is to write your proposal so that your mother can understand it, even if she is not a schoolteacher.

In good writing there is no substitute for clarity–not big words, not sentence length, not type style or size. The easier your proposal is to read, the more likely it will be thoroughly read. The harder you make it for the reader to understand your project, the less likely it is that your plan will be read, understood, and funded. Think *USA Today*.

Hook Your Reader from the Beginning

One of your objectives should be to clearly establish who you are and what your goals are. Tell the reader why you have credibility in the project area you are proposing; then lead directly into the statement of need. Write simply and to the point. Shine the spotlight on your ideas.

There is no time like the beginning to capture the reader's interest. Start with a powerful image for the need you propose to fill or a persuasive testimonial or quote from a student. Provide concrete examples. Your objective is to show the reader why your project or idea is unique.

Another way to capture the reader's attention is to begin with a question. "How can one school library make a difference in the digital divide? At Sunny Skies School library, we think we have an answer . . ."

Define Terms

If you are going to use an educational term, define it initially in as few words as possible and illustrate with an example. For instance, "*Service learning* is a teaching method that combines service to a community with a standard K-12 academic curriculum. As part of their schoolwork, students perform community projects in order to build both academic skills and civic responsibility."

If you need to use technical terms, do not assume your reader understands them. Translate them into ordinary language. Team members who review grant proposals come from a variety of fields. While another school librarian might know just what you mean, a coordinator of vocational technical programs may not.

Spell Out Acronyms the First Time

If you want to refer in your proposal to your library media center as the LMC, start by spelling the words in full followed by the acronym in parentheses. Subsequently throughout the document, you may refer to it as the LMC. Beware of using too many acronyms. The lay reader has a hard time with alphabet soup. While you may know that ELL refers to students who are English Language Learners, assume that your grant reader has never heard the term before.

Avoid Jargon

It is easy for educators to get into the habit of using educational jargon. When they begin to speak in the jargon of their profession, noneducators can be clueless. While to an educator, *special education* may mean a specific educational program mandated by law for students who have an individualized educational program (IEP), those words may mean nothing specific to a lay grant application reader. To avoid having to define too many terms, stay away from jargon. If you mean *school*, use the word *school*, not *attendance center*.

Make It Simply the Best

The person assigned to read and score your grant proposal probably has a stack of several grant proposals to read and score. Do him a favor by keeping yours easy to read. Picture in your mind motivational, high-interest/low-vocabulary books. Hold that mental picture when writing your grant. Make your proposal a high-interest, easy-to-read document.

The reader isn't interested in how intelligent the grant writer is or what big words she knows. He wants to know what the money is needed for, what is going to be done for the students with that money, and what the plan to measure the results is.

Make sure there is plenty of meat on the bones of your proposal; leave the fat for another project. Picture yourself writing a lean and enduring proposal using short, meaningful sentences. More pages and multi-syllabic words do not equate with a better chance at funding. Keep your proposal simple and crystal clear. Your reader will value your brevity and precision.

Avoid Redundancy, Clichés, and Fluff

As you make your case, say it once and say it well. Saying the same thing six different ways does not endear yourself to your reader. Be aware that the proposal may ask you for the information in more than one section. Furnish the information in each section where it is requested, modifying but not embellishing the language. Proofread to eliminate repetition.

Again, remember not to make the same point over and over again until your reader is sick of hearing about the point that you are making. Try not to be redundant and say things over and over again. The reader gets really tired of reading when you make the same point over and over again. Remember, do not be redundant or say the same things over and over again. Get our point?

Find Synonyms

Reread what you have written. Are you using the same tired words over and over? Can you find suitable synonyms for them? Use the thesaurus on your software. Do not beat a dead horse, feel the benefactor's pain, or smell the roses. Avoid using words like *nice*, *great*, *fun*, *wonderful,* and *absolutely*; they are overused and tired. As you edit your first draft you will probably find that you have included a few clichés and some tired words. What do you really mean? Take the trouble to find the precise adjective, an original metaphor. It is hard to be trite when you are being scrupulously specific.

Provide Examples

They make your grant proposal come alive. When you paint a vivid picture with your words you put some fizz in your proposal. If you want computer laptop labs with Internet access for your students, describe the students surfing the NASA site to learn about science experiments in space. Then show how the students, as a result of this project, will become more proficient in science. Hollywood claims that nothing sells a story like a child or a dog. You have the children. Use them to sell your idea. Grantors want to know that their money will make a difference in the lives of children.

Avoid sounding arrogant or overconfident. Do not talk down to the reader or try to obfuscate something that you would prefer the reader not discern. Avoid using controversial language.

Consider Your Reader

Just as some people talk too much, some people use too many words when writing. Say what needs to be said, but leave out the fluff and the filler. When a proposal has been stuffed with jargon and padded with verbiage, the alert reader wonders, "Where's the beef?" Substance yes—window dressing no. Words are telling and readers are bright.

Use a Consistent Style and Format

Find a Voice

Find your writer's voice and use it consistently throughout the grant proposal. Avoid switching from first person to second person to third person and back again.

If you are fortunate enough to have a team writing the proposal, one person must take on the job of putting the several contributions into one voice. The final document should read as though it were written from start to finish by one person. Achieving this uniform voice is difficult, but without it you jeopardize your proposal's credibility.

Speak Clearly

Use precise language. Take the newspaper *USA Today* as a model. Their writers write so that the average citizen can read and comprehend. Erudition and extensive matriculation are impressive in graduate school. Plain speaking goes a long way with an overburdened grant reader. Make clarity and precision your goals.

Use the active voice. Instead of "The run was scored by Big Rex," write, "Big Rex scored the run!"

Transition Words, Phrases for Coherence

Use all the tips your former English teachers taught you in order to help your reader follow your train of thought. Begin each new section with a strong introductory sentence and wording that tells the reader where it fits in your overall plan. For instance, "Our third indicator that something needed to be done came in the spring of 2009. . . .". As you move from paragraph to paragraph and section to section, provide transition words and phrases: *first, next, and then, finally.*

Think of alternate ways to say something that must be repeated. Linking expressions are numerous: *in conclusion, to conclude, to sum up, finally, in short, hence, therefore, furthermore, another, moreover, at last.*

Use connecting words to show the relationship between ideas, details and sections of your proposal. Some common transitional words and phrases are

after	*after that*	*also*
another	*as a result*	*at the same time*
besides	*consequently*	*finally*
for example	*for instance*	*however*
in addition	*instead*	*later*
likewise	*otherwise*	*similarly*

Use the Language of the Grantor

This is a favorite grant-writing tip. As you carefully read the grant application, remember that you highlighted the key words or phrases your potential benefactor used. Now is the time to incorporate those words within your own proposal. When members of the grant review committee spot those words, they will sense they have a winner. Bing, bing, bing, fifty points!

Describe or State Precisely

How could you say, "A lot of students will benefit greatly" in a more precise manner? Could you say, "All 537 students at Happy Days School will be scheduled to use the laptop computer lab a minimum of one hour per week to practice their writing skills?"

It is critical to be specific in your budget section. The donor cares deeply how grant funds will be spent. For example, *"Travel - $500"* does not paint an accurate picture. *"Purchase round trip airline tickets at $250 each for two authors to travel from Jonesville to Springfield in April"* is much clearer. Specificity in budget writing is supremely important.

Be Compelling and Fresh

The grantor and the grant application reader are human beings. While your proposal must present the facts, you must also persuade the reader to choose your project for funding. Humanize your proposal, but do not go overboard. Put some emotion in the draft without making it a sob story. Use dramatic details that illuminate the situation you are describing. Avoid exaggeration and overstatement. Do not promise more than your project can deliver.

Find a way to allow your personality, your heart, and your energy to shine through your words without overpowering your good ideas. After a reviewer reads so many proposals, the words on the page can begin to look like "blah, blah, blah." If your commitment to your students and community are genuine, find a way to let that energy and commitment shine through.

Readers love a surprise or a puzzle when it is presented well. It provides a mental oasis in a desert of dry proposals. After reading a number of grant applications, the reader becomes numb to the standard pattern of the document. The art of grant writing makes a difference when the writer adds something that makes a proposal resonate with the reader.

Appearance Does Matter

The layout of your proposal can also make a powerful statement about your organizational skills and clarity of thought.

Graphics

Many readers prefer graphic representations of complex ideas. Use a chart, graph, or timeline to demonstrate your concept whenever possible. You can save words and clarify complex descriptions by using a well-done graphic.

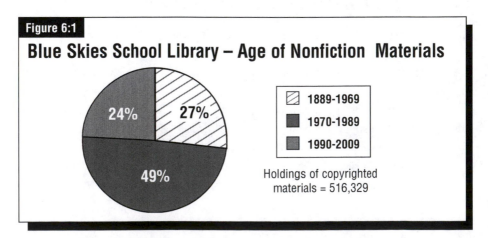

Figure 6:1

Blue Skies School Library – Age of Nonfiction Materials

- 1889-1969
- 1970-1989
- 1990-2009

27%
24%
49%

Holdings of copyrighted materials = 516,329

Paint a clear picture with the statistics; don't put the reader to sleep. Use bullets and charts instead of wordy sentences to show your needs.

A time-and-task chart can be helpful to demonstrate project activities and timeline. Consider searching for a graphic organizer that will help your reader better understand your ideas.

White Space

Plan to provide your overworked proposal reader with plenty of white space. Use headings and subheadings and make them **bold**. Avoid underlining or using ALL CAPITAL LETTERS or *italics*. Those devices all make a document more difficult to read.

White space makes it easier for the reader to skim for important details. Leaving plenty of white space in your document makes your proposal more reader- friendly and sends mental signals that one topic or section is ending and another is beginning. White space provides transition space for the reader's brain to shift from one unit of information to another. Beware; the dense underbrush of too many words can bury your good ideas.

> *Beware; the dense underbrush of too many words can bury your good ideas.*

Lists and Headings

One way you can provide white space and get your reader to focus on the main point is to use lists. Lists make it easier for the reader to skim the sections of your proposal. Use a numbered list when items need to be understood in a specific order. Use bullets if sequence is not significant. Lists can save you words, and that is critical if there is a word limit for your proposal.

Headings help the reader keep a sense of order. They act as graphic organizers and help the reader go quickly back to previous information when a question arises. Headings are a courtesy to the reader; they open the door to the next section. They help maintain adequate white space and show that you respect the reader's valuable time.

After the reviewer has read a proposal once, she usually needs to read it again. Having subject headings and subheadings in place allows her to skim the document for necessary information—almost like a table of contents to the hurried reader.

Headings and subheadings should always match the headings in the RFP, where applicable. If you have the grantor's scoring rubric as part of the application, you can see where the reviewer will be awarding points. Make sure your subject headings correspond to that rubric and stand out. In other words, help the reviewer decide in your favor.

Spacing and Margins

Double spacing is standard for grant proposals unless the guidelines request otherwise. Double spacing provides the reader with more white space for clarity and readability. Single-spaced lines are difficult to read, more likely to produce headaches and eyestrain, and leave no space for the reviewer to write comments.

Unless otherwise specified, leave the right margins ragged. Do not "right align" the text in the body of your proposal. Right-alignment produces irregular spacing within the line, and that is distracting to the reader. Ragged right margins make reading easier.

Font, Type Size, and Pagination

Type size should be large enough to read comfortably; 12-point is standard. Tiny print may allow you to get more words into your proposal, but those words won't do you much good if the reader can't read them. Check the grant application specifications carefully for required type size. If none is given, use no smaller than 10 points. Do your best to make the document comfortable for the eye of the reader.

The type style, or font, may be stipulated in the proposal guidelines. If it is not, use a common, standard, easy-to-read serif font. Avoid sans serif fonts as they are more difficult to read. Type style is not a place to be highly original. Save the swirly o's and squiggle letters for your scrapbook, not a formal grant proposal.

The pages of your proposal should be numbered. Page numbers are most easily read when they are at bottom center or at top right of the page. Do not number the title page or the first page of the document. Use an alternative pagination system such as lower-case Roman numerals for the appendix and table of contents.

Avoid Fancy

Do not be tempted to put bells and whistles in your proposal. Although you want your proposal to stand out from the rest, you want it to stand on the merit of its content, not its shiny red cover and micro chip that plays "Jingle Bells" when the cover is open. Save fancy notebooks, folders, and bindings for your family albums.

Big notebooks or three-ring binders can be a nuisance to the receiver. They are more expensive to mail and difficult for the recipient to store. The grant proposal should follow the grantor's guidelines and be stapled or paper-clipped just as requested.

Tip: Add Pagination

Add pagination when you are editing. Bottom center of each page or upper right-hand corner are the prime spots for page numbers.

Plan Ahead

Writing a winning proposal takes time. Give yourself the luxury of plenty of time to write, edit, and rewrite your proposal. If you know that a grant competition's deadline is one year away, you would be wise to begin preliminary work to put your proposal together. If you hear about a competition that is due two weeks from today, applying for it is probably not a viable option for this round. Writing a grant takes time. Allow yourself about three months to write a first draft, edit, and revise.

To summarize:

- Hook the reader at the start.
- Define terms; spell out acronyms at first mention.
- Avoid jargon, redundancy, clichés, filler, and fluff.
- Use short sentences.
- Be brief, precise, and say it once.
- Use transitions to keep your reader with you.
- Choose meaningful words and give clear examples.
- Use relevant statistics.
- Speak the language of your prospective benefactor.
- Keep visual concerns in mind.
- List and highlight; use consistent formatting.
- Take a fresh approach.
- Reread and revise.
- Use your language skills to make your grant stand out from others.

Chapter 7

Edit Until It Hurts

It requires more than mere genius to be an author.

— Jean De La Bruyere

The First Draft

Get your ideas written down, make sure you have met the RFP's guidelines, and then put your first draft aside for a day or two. This way, you'll reread it with fresh eyes as you start to revise. You will need to read and revise it several times before you are ready to take it to the editor.

Read, Reread, Write, and Rewrite

Once a proposal is written, it is necessary to read it over and over again. If you are doing your job properly, you will have read and reread it so many times that you've begun to memorize it. If you can put it aside for a few days between readings, you'll find each time that you've left out something pertinent.

You will also rewrite several times. Do not be discouraged. Remember, writing is a process, and rewriting is an important facet of it. You will improve your document each time you revise it.

Title It. A catchy title is a major asset to your proposal. *Hola Dr. Seuss* was the title of a winning application from a media specialist who wanted Spanish language books for her elementary library. *Spanish Language Books for the Highlands Media Center* just doesn't carry the cachet of *Hola Dr. Seuss*. The proposal review team continually referred back to *Hola Dr. Seuss* as they considered the projects. The title was catchy and easy to remember. It hooked the readers. They smiled as they repeated it, "*Hola Dr. Seuss*," again and again during the review process.

Headings and Lists. Look for ways to put in meaningful headings and subheadings. They help the reader see at a glance the organization of your paper and spot the main points.

Read again to see if you can eliminate long sentences by making lists. For example, "We will gather input from

- Students,
- Staff,
- Parents,
- Administration, and
- Community."

Tip: Write and Rewrite

In order to produce a quality grant proposal, it will be necessary to write and rewrite the proposal several times. Writing is a process, and rewriting is a vital facet of that process. It is important to get the first draft done before the rewrite begins. Metaphorically speaking, let it get cool before you slice-and-dice.

Revise It for Mechanics and Content

Let a few days go by and read the manuscript again to see if you can reduce it, rearrange it, and rewrite it to improve its clarity. Ask an educator to proofread and edit your proposal. Educators are great at finding errors and can also help with content suggestions.

Flesh It Out

As you reread it, you will see where more flesh is needed on the bones of your proposal and where there are holes in your argument. Where would an example help make your points? Add substance until the proposal is clear and convincing even to someone completely outside your field.

Give It Punch

Find a way to make your grant proposal stand out from the rest. You cannot print your grant on colored paper, but you can use colorful language. You can tell a powerful story and hook your reader. Remember how a good murder mystery captures your attention from the first page by delivering a juicy murder right off? Blast off with a personal story, a colorful example, or a question.

Make the necessary statistics interesting. Clarify your argument with statistics, but don't put the reader to sleep. A testimonial from a fellow teacher, a quote from a student, or a note of thanks from a parent could make your proposal come to life. A powerful opening is part of what persuades reviewers to select a project for funding.

Be Specific; Let the Narrative Flow

Avoid generalities such as *a lot*, *many*, *really big*, and other nonspecific words and phrases. Too many generalities make your proposal float in a sea of words. Anchor your points with solid information and precise language.

Read your proposal aloud to yourself. Does it flow smoothly? If not, could you improve the transitions from topic to topic, section to section? Does the rhythm of your words make you stumble? Are like ideas expressed in parallel structures? Revise until the narrative flows.

You Cannot Overdo Proofreading

Read your proposal again and again, looking at it each time from a different aspect. Look for content. Is your proposal beefy enough, or do you need to add substance and weight?

What about the mechanics? Put on your best English-teacher glasses and look for split infinitives, faulty parallelism, passive voice, subject-verb agreement problems, and spelling errors. How about typos? Did you type *you* when you meant *your*? Have you used antonyms correctly? How about *there*, *their*, and *they're* and *to*, *too*, and *two*?

You selected your words with great care, but once more, reread your draft for word choice. Did you use the same tired words repeatedly? Try once more to find suitable synonyms for them.

Remember that thesaurus in your software? Use it to check nuances of meaning and to find synonyms for words you've overused. That old grammar or composition textbook may still come in handy. If in doubt on a point of style, consult the *Publication Manual of the American Psychological Association*, the accepted style guide for many grant proposal writers. Another great choice is Purdue's OWL site at <http://owl.english.purdue.edu/>.

How about tone? Ask a friend to read it and tell you if it sounds arrogant, overconfident, or condescending—a definite turn-off to your prospective reader.

Proofread for the logic of your argument. Have you stated the need coherently and provided enough research to support your plan? Is the argument persuasive, or do you need to add an example and cite an authority?

Your finished proposal should be so polished it is ready for publication. How your proposal looks and reads is a critical measurement of your professional skills.

Even though proposal-writing is probably not part of the project for which you are seeking funding, it is what the grantor has to use to gauge your credibility.

Try an experiment. Let your proposal sit awhile, then come back to read it again. Did your key message come through when you read it? Did you feel the power of the argument? If not, get to work revising it until your message is clear. Ask yourself: If you were the reviewer, would you remember the title of your grant proposal? Would you remember its essence? If you can honestly say yes, then you have met the goal for substance.

Two Essentials: An Editor and a Proofreader

Now it is time to put your proposal before more objective eyes. Do not try to be your own editor. If you've written a good proposal, a professional editor can make it great. Ideally, you'll be part of a writing team that includes an editor. If you don't have that luxury, do not worry. You still need an editor.

If possible, get help from both within and outside your organization. Could you volunteer to help a colleague with a project in exchange for having him edit yours?

Especially after several rereadings, our brains fill in words that are not really there. Here's where a proofreader comes in. Find a peer who will proofread as well as one who will edit for you—people whom you can trust to care for and nurture your brainchild. Give the proofreader a copy of the RFP so that she can also watch for procedural errors.

Ask questions of your proofreader and editor:

- What did you not understand?
- Where do I need to include more information?
- Where does the proposal sound repetitive?
- Which parts are too technical?
- Where is the proposal confusing?

If possible, hire a freelance editor or consultant to proofread or edit your manuscript. The local community college or university may refer you to someone who can proof, edit, and revise.

Follow Directions to the Letter

Following directions is essential in grant writing. When you serve as a grant reader, you will find it surprising how many grant writers fail to follow the directions. Nothing will end your funding chances faster than failing to do what the directions say. If you are a rebel at heart, get a body part pierced or choose a funky hair color but follow the grantor's guidelines to the letter. Doing all this hard work only to be eliminated in the first round is demoralizing.

Grant proposals that do not meet the specified criteria do not make it to the finals. If the proposal states that no "bricks-and-mortar" be funded and you ask for a greenhouse attachment for your media center, you will be rejected.

If the proposal says you may include a specified maximum number of attachments, then follow the directions. If it specifies that the abstract must be limited to one page, then don't make it a page and a half. If the specs say you may not request personnel, don't ask for funding for a library clerk. If you must have three letters of support, then include three, not two or four.

Meet the deadline—no excuses. If you miss the deadline, your proposal will not be considered.

Use a Checklist

You will need a checklist when you are ready to complete your proposal. Include on it all the pertinent information that you have highlighted in the RFP. Go over each section carefully. It might include the following:

- Follow application guidelines.
- Proofread.
- Attach required documents.
- Sign all required forms.
- Submit requested number of copies.
- Meet all deadlines.

If you are allowed to do so, place the title on a header or footer on each page of your proposal. Do not reveal the name of your school or district within the body of the proposal if the guidelines forbid it.

Check the Budget with the Proposal and the Business Office

Did you complete your budget and then make changes in your proposal plan? If so, did you change the budget to reflect the changes in the plan? Have you checked the math again and again?

Have you met with the powers-that-be in your district business office? Are they aware of your proposal and supportive of it? Will they have a way of receiving your funds, should you get them, and dispersing them appropriately? Have you dotted all the i's and crossed the t's, just the way the business office likes you to do?

Signatures

Do you have all the required signatures? Do you need an appointment with the superintendent or principal to get his signature? Be sure all copies of your proposal have the requisite signatures. Don't allow all your hard work to go for naught by forgetting to get a required signature and having your project rejected on a technicality. It can be heartbreaking to wait until the last minute and then learn that the superintendent is out of town and not expected back until after your deadline. Plan ahead and get yourself on the calendar of the people who will need to sign your proposal.

If you are doing your homework properly, the signatures will be more than a last-minute formality. You will have kept the key people affected by your project in the information loop. Each of them will have a clear picture of what your project entails and will have good reason to be supportive. Each will have reviewed the final copy and approved your plan. The signatures will be just the final step.

Appendices

Gather all the necessary documents for inclusion in the appendices. If you are working with cooperating organizations, do you have the necessary material from them?

One of the grant proposals we wrote required a copy of our district's five-year plan and technology plan. Both were large and cumbersome documents. The state required several copies of the grant proposal, including the appendices. One time-consuming job was to get those plans copied and ready for inclusion.

Other appendices that may be required are:

- A list of other funding sources,
- Financial statements,
- Resumes, curricula vitae, or biographies of your project team,
- Current budget information,
- Articles about your school or project,
- Equipment specifications,
- Verification of tax-exempt status,
- Photos or news clippings, and
- Endorsements or testimonials.

Keep copies of your appendices as well as of your proposal.

Cover Letter

Do you need a cover letter? Have you written it on your school or district's letterhead? Is it addressed to the proper recipient?

Copies

Usually, the RFP will ask for duplicate or triplicate copies of your application. You will need a copy of the proposal and appendices for:

- each member of your grant-writing team,
- your principal,
- your superintendent,

- cooperating colleagues and agencies, and
- the file.

Make more copies than you think you will need. When you are making eight copies of a document, it is easier to make nine than it is to go back and put the whole thing on the copier again. If you are copying newspaper articles for inclusion, cut and paste them to fit nicely on a page. Enlarge or reduce as necessary. Make sure you get the necessary permissions before copying copyrighted materials.

Make sure your copies are clear and legible. If the copier is leaving odd marks on the document, take it to another copier. The appearance of your proposal is very important.

Making the copies of the proposal will be one of the last tasks on your list. Last-minute changes do occur, so wait to copy the document until all signatures are on it and all changes have been made.

Assembly

Fasten each of your document sections with paper clips, binder clips, or staples unless the directions call for some other method of assembly. Do not use a binder unless the RFP requests that you do.

Carefully following the guidelines, you are going to place your cover letter, your proposal, and your appendices in a manila envelope. Put the packet together in an organized and attractive manner.

Address the envelope to the correct person at the right address. Make your return address legible. You may want to insert an 8 1/2-inch by 11-inch piece of cardboard in the envelope to keep the pages stable.

If the guidelines are not clear, call or e-mail the agency and see if someone there can help you with specific guidelines for assembling and mailing your proposal. Do not include materials that were not requested. Respect the grantor's requests.

Mailing

You must decide on the best method for getting your proposal to its destination. Ideally, you will have completed your application in plenty of time to send it by first class mail. If not, non-government delivery companies offer quick service. But consider what it says to the potential benefactor if you use an expensive delivery service. Are you being a good steward of your limited funds? The grantor expects you to be a careful spender. A good tip is to send it with receipt of confirmation and tracking options, when possible. If your submission is electronic, be prepared to follow the directions to the letter. You will probably need a pin number and username, and you may need to put your proposal in PDF format. Be sure to get and file the receipt notification. Confirmation that your proposal has been received is critical. Many funders will allow you to check the status of your submission online.

Editing your proposal and carefully following directions are not very glamorous activities, but they pay off well. Check your proposal once more. Have you:

- Revised and rewritten your first draft?
- Given your project a catchy title?
- Put "punch" in your proposal?
- Written a cover letter?
- Found editing and proofreading help?
- Followed directions to the letter?
- Checked with the business office?
- Gotten signatures?
- Attached the appendices?
- Made copies?

Congratulations!

You and your team have completed a major project. The proposal is in the mail. What an accomplishment! It is time to recognize and thank all who have helped.

Chapter 8

Turn Rejection into Success

When one door is shut, another one opens.
— Miguel de Cervantes, Don Quixote

I t is wise to have a talk with yourself after you send off your grant application. It may take months before you hear from the grantor. Are you prepared to be patient? And to accept the decision, either way it goes?

Grace is required, whether your project is placed in the winner's circle or outside it. If your project is funded, you will want to sing it from the rooftops. If the word is not positive, you may wish that the fleas of a thousand camels would infest the grant review team. Neither is a good choice.

Never, ever condemn or berate a potential grantor or a proposal review board. Do not even think about calling the grantor if you are feeling hurt, rejected, or hostile.

Spend some time in front of the mirror, practicing a graceful statement that lets your team know that the project was not funded.

Be Professional

You may feel as if you need a good cry or a little chocolate if you get a "Dear John" letter from the grantor. It is fine to have that moment of down time, but try to have it in the privacy of your own home and family or with your best friend. Put on your best professional face for your administrator, your team members, and your community. You have done a difficult and admirable thing; you have written a grant application. Be proud of your accomplishment.

If you are notified that your grant was not funded, you have permission to feel just a moment or two of rejection. But that is just about all the down time you get. Do not take the rejection personally. Get back up, dust yourself off, and try again.

Experts say that only about one proposal in 10 is funded. It is possible to write a perfect application and still not have it funded.

You put a lot of work into that grant proposal. That effort is not for naught. People succeed, not projects. Just the act of working together as a team with your faculty is a unifying force for your school. The energy created by collaborating with others gives momentum to your school improvement plan. Identifying needs and solutions, as you have done in writing the grant proposal, can lead to increased support from your school system and community, whether the proposed project is funded or not.

Stay calm. Keep your sense of direction and your determination to get what is best for your students. It takes effort, time, and patience to win grant money. Just completing a grant proposal is an effort worthy of commendation.

Notify Your Team

Remember those wonderful people who worked with you to put this proposal together? They, too, are waiting to hear the news. Your administrator, your staff, your grant-writing team, your editor and proofreader, your volunteers, your collaborating entities, and your students are waiting for word from you.

As soon as you can tell them in a dignified and appropriate manner, get to each of your support team and let them know the bad news. If you plan to revise and resubmit in the next round, let them know that too. Tell them how much you appreciated their help and support.

Thank Participants

There is nothing like a handwritten thank-you note for each of your project participants and supporters. Take the time to sit down and write a personal note to each of your team members, thanking her or him for giving time and talent to this project.

Do not forget to thank the grantor, even though your project was not selected. This is an opportunity to build a lasting relationship. Express your appreciation for the person's or organization's philanthropy. Thank the grantor for giving you the opportunity to apply.

Reasons for Rejection

Was your abstract clear? Did you follow directions? Was the budget request reasonable? What can you learn about your application that will enable you to revise and resubmit it? Revision is far less work than starting from scratch. After some time passes, it is easier to get the proposal back out and look at it from a new perspective.

While reasons vary on why your grant might not have been funded, here are some common reasons for rejection.

Precision Fit

The most frequent reason proposals fail is that they do not match the grantor's specifications or vision. Carefully reading both the application guidelines and the background information about the grantor should help you avoid this error.

Bridesmaid, Not a Bride

You followed the guidelines but your proposal did not have the "right stuff" to put you on the winners' pile. Get feedback from someone who has written winning grant proposals. Have a buddy read your proposal and tell you what is great about it and what is not. Then bite the bullet and rewrite your grant proposal. Somehow, you just did not "click" with this particular funder.

Budget Buster

In the eyes of the grantor, you may have asked for too much money for too small an impact on too few students. Or she may have felt that your budget was too small to make a significant difference for students. Did the grantor set a $150 limit, and you asked for $1,500?

Ask for constructive criticism from the person who notifies you that you were not funded. Sometimes reviewers are reluctant to give you feedback, so be polite and eager to learn; do not challenge their judgment or ask for a point recount.

Me, Me, Me

Could it be that what you have asked for in your grant proposal benefits the media specialists more than the students? While donors probably like you and want to support you, they want to put their money where the students are. While an extra computer in your workroom for you to use exclusively for management might be ideal, the grantor probably will not see it as having a significant impact on students.

Not Needy Enough

You may not have painted a vivid enough picture of your students' needs. While your project idea may be sound, you have to be crystal clear about the needs of your students. Make the grant-giver feel their pain. Show how funding your proposal will have lasting impact on their lives.

Unwanted Proposal

The odds for success are slim when you send a proposal to a grantor who has not asked for it. As in the publishing world, "over-the-transom" submissions have little chance. A letter or call to the granting agency will tell you if you are applying to a likely source or not.

Insufficient Documentation

Does your proposal state that you are working cooperatively with the local community college but lack any documentation of that collaboration?

Frivolous Request

Have you asked for a luxury like a reading loft for your library when there are children in your community who lack basic necessities like books on their library shelves?

Too Much for Too Few

Have you asked for a lot of money to benefit a few students? Donors like to support projects that make sweeping, vast differences in the lives of as many people as possible. Again, collaborating with others will help broaden your base and improve your chances of funding.

Impossible Dream

Have you claimed that a storytelling workshop will increase your school's reading scores by 5 percent? Make sure you can support such a claim with research and statistics.

Weak Writing

Face it. Some proposals are not written well, are hard to follow, or lack the power to persuade. The writer may have left out critical information or documentation. The budget may have errors or lack necessary information. Experts say that many grant proposals are rejected because they are poorly written. If you suspect that is why your request was turned down, this is a fixable problem. Seek help.

More reasons for rejection:
- The funding source did not solicit the proposal.
- The proposed project would not serve the grantor's target group.
- The proposal is poorly written and confusing to read.
- You have not convinced the grantor of the project designer's qualifications.
- The proposal's budget is too big, too small, or filled with errors.

- The evaluation plan is weak or nonexistent.
- There is no evidence the plan can be sustained when the project is over.
- The proposal didn't follow the RFP guidelines.
- The grant-seeker's mission and the grant-giver's mission are not in sync.
- The goals are too lofty or too vague.
- The project sounds risky.

Learn from the Experience

You can make the necessary revisions and submit your grant on the next funding round. Go on to land the big one next time, once you have assimilated the information about your current proposal. Remember the little train who thought he could. Don't give up when you are almost at the top of the mountain. Get that proposal off the shelf and look for another potential fund source. Review the progress you have made so far and make a plan to get feedback, modify your proposal, and try again.

- Consider taking a class on grant writing.
- Communicate with your team the status of your proposal.
- Try other donors.
- Get feedback.
- Analyze the reasons your proposal wasn't selected.
- Ask to read a winning proposal.
- Get back up on the horse that bucked you.

Feedback Helps

Accept rejection as a learning experience, gather up your courage, and ask for feedback. Can you find out why your proposal was not selected? Was it too similar to another? Was the budget in line with the grantor's vision?

Do not be discouraged if your proposal is not funded on the first try. Remember Colonel Sanders sold his recipe on the 1,009th try.

When you ask for feedback, listen carefully. What you hear might make the difference you need to be funded the next time. Think about the feedback for a while. Turn it over in your mind and try to see the criticism from a perspective other than your own. When you have put a lot of hard work into a project, it is natural to defend something so near and dear to your heart. But do not reject criticism; try to learn from it instead.

Take a Class

If your grant was not funded on its first submission, consider taking a grant-writing class either online or face-to-face or attending a grant-writing seminar before you revise your proposal. This may be a better time to take a course than when you were writing under a deadline. The instructor's words will have more meaning now that you have navigated the waters of grant-writing. Many grant sources offer funding opportunities cyclically. After attending a seminar or taking an online course or Webinar, you may feel inspired to revise and resubmit your proposal for the next round of competition.

Read a Winner

Ask the grantor's project manager if you may read one of the proposals selected for funding. Read it carefully. Send a thank-you note for the grantor's courtesy. If you cannot read a successful proposal of a fellow applicant, find some examples on the Internet. Print them out and study them. See examples on the CD. We all need to see and understand a good model before we can hope to produce a winning entry ourselves.

Try Again

Remember all those famous people who suffered rejection and still eventually succeeded? How many times did Lincoln run for office before he was elected? How many times are authors rejected before they sell their first best seller?

It was reported that Einstein did not speak until age three. A newspaper editor fired Walt Disney for lacking imagination. Babe Ruth struck out 1,300 times—a Major League record.

Persevere. Stick to your guns. You can do it. What if Orville and Wilbur had given up after their first failure? We would not be squeezing ourselves into those comfy seats and flying off to fabulous library conferences.

Revise and Recycle

 Plan A might be to resubmit the grant proposal to the same entity in the next funding cycle, after editing and revising it. Be sure you get any available feedback from the review of your proposal; try to learn which sections did well and which need help.

Recycling an old grant is much easier than writing a new one. Even recycling an already funded grant to a new grantor is easy. Consider your grant, once written, an asset. You can bring it out, overhaul it, and resubmit it multiple times. Resubmitting a revised version of a non-funded proposal can bring a good return on your investment of time and effort.

It is possible for a media specialist to get funding from two and three grant sources for the same project. A worthwhile project has lasting, universal appeal. If your grant-funded summer institute was terrific one summer, it could be so again another summer, made possible by a totally different sponsor.

If your lifelong dream is to read illuminated manuscripts at the Bodleian in Oxford, don't give up at the first rejection. Find out what your proposal scored in each of the sections. Reflect on your weak areas and brainstorm ways to strengthen them. Rework your proposal and resubmit it the next round. Many grants are offered twice a year, most annually, and there is usually no restriction on submitting a revised edition of last year's proposal. Editing, reworking, and rethinking increase your chances of making your dreams come true.

Applying to More Than One Grantor

With a little research, you may find other grant sources to whom you could submit the same proposal with very little modification. If you do submit the same proposal at the same time to more than one fund source, you should communicate that in your project proposal information.

Many large projects are funded by multiple funding sources. Events such as writer's conferences require so much funding and planning that they typically have more than one benefactor. It makes good sense to develop a grant proposal that can be modified or customized for specific money sources.

Chapter 9

Celebrate and Share

Success, remember, is the reward of toil.

— **Sophocles**

Y ou have just received a grant! Congratulations and best wishes! It is time to celebrate with those who helped make this achievement possible. Personally contact each team member (as well as your boss and superintendent, of course) to share the good news. Let faculty, students, and parents know about it. They will be proud. Call your colleagues at the collaborating institutions.

Next, send a letter of appreciation to your benefactors. Be sure to let them know how thrilled you are and that you are ready to hit the ground running with your project.

Elation, Then Letdown

A letdown feeling may take you by surprise when you hang up the phone after hearing that you have won a grant. You have worked so hard writing your grant and have invested so much time that you're out of steam.

Or you may have written and submitted the grant so long ago that you had almost forgotten it when you were notified of winning. You may find yourself neck deep in alligators of another variety like a construction project, state testing, or an all-school flu epidemic. You may ask yourself, "What was I thinking when I asked for this grant?"

Allow yourself to feel a little overwhelmed, overworked, and out of steam. The feeling will pass and your energy will return, but many veteran grant writers confess to feeling a moment's regret when they get what they asked for. After all, winning a grant means getting an opportunity to work extra hours and feel more pressure and stress. If you encounter these feelings, remember that very soon they will be replaced with a sense of joy and celebration. You will be accomplishing something worthwhile for your students and your school community. It is worth all the hard work to see those test scores rise and your students turn into avid readers.

Get the Word Out

Your stock will be high when the world knows about your Midas touch. The maxim that the rich get richer is true in the world of grants. Once you have the aura of having gotten grant money, people will see you in a new light—a golden light. Perception is reality. When the world knows you received a grant, it will be much easier to get the second one and the one after that. Picture that on your curriculum vitae!

Share the Limelight

Do not allow yourself be the focus of all the media attention. Spread the accolades among all the participants. Acknowledge your benefactor every chance you get. The grantor justifiably expects to receive a public relations benefit from his largesse. Most philanthropists, though, have a larger goal: finding a solution to a vexing problem and then disseminating the findings far and wide so as to positively affect the lives of many. Sharing your project with others is a type of civic duty.

Everyone likes positive publicity, including the superintendent of your school district and the mayor of your town. Your winning grant can provide many opportunities to highlight the progress of your school, library, district, students, staff, and families.

Keep a Scrapbook or Portfolio

Once you have won a grant, make a permanent record of your success in a standard three-ring binder and a package of plastic sheet protectors or a computer file of scanned and saved items. Include things, such as:

- The grant proposal,
- The notification letter telling you the good news about funding,
- Each of the press releases about your grant,
- Pictures of the participants and events,

- Newspaper and journal clippings, and
- Journal articles about your project.

Continue to put clippings, photos, and other memorabilia in your scrapbook, real or virtual, throughout the life of the project. This will be an historic record of the project and provide a treasure trove of information when others, such as the press, have questions or ask for photos and other records of your project. It will also help you as you plan and write more grant proposals.

Share the good news:

Within Your School

Start your dissemination program right at home. Your project can be shared with your staff on staff development days, school improvement meeting days, in mentoring sessions with student teachers and new teachers, and informally in the teacher's lunchroom.

Web Page. Post your grant success stories on your library Web page. What a great way to spread the word about your grant within your school community as well as throughout the world.

Posters. Make a poster (or ask your creative students to do it) for your media center showing what your grant is doing for your library. Did you get money to buy books and backpacks for your preschoolers? Take photos of the children at school and at home reading with parents, and showcase them on a colorful poster.

Bookmarks. Make bookmarks about your project and place them on your circulation desk.

Share In the Local Community

Contact the local news media through:

Press Releases. If your school system has a communications expert or a public relations specialist, give her a call to share the news about your grant. She will probably want to write a press release about it. She is likely to have distribution lists and media contacts that will gain maximum exposure for you, your benefactor, and your project. If you don't have a public relations person, get your principal's permission to write a press release yourself and send it to local newspapers and radio and TV stations. A timely e-mail or fax of a press release each time your project enters a new phase is a sure way to keep your venture in the news. Some funding agencies will provide press releases for you.

News Conferences. A significant grant may call for a news conference. Your school district administrators will determine if that is appropriate. Let your grant-writing teammates answer some of the questions.

Additionally, you can share your good news through:

Newsletters. Write a story for your school newsletter as soon as you've received the good news. Your colleagues, your students, and their parents will want to know. Give them a succinct account of what you have gotten, from whom, and for what purpose. This is another opportunity to give credit and express appreciation to the grantor.

PTA/PTO Meetings. Make sure your PTA or PTO is "in the loop" and ask to be placed on the agenda of its next meeting for a short presentation describing your grant project. Be sure and thank PTA for its support of your media center as you share the good news.

Among Your Peers

Let your associations and professional affiliations know about your good news.

Associations. The teacher's association; your local, state and national library associations; and fraternities may want to highlight your good fortune through their listserv, online journals, and other communications.

Journals. *School Library Journal* wants photos of your library hosting special events or kicking off special occasions. Send your photos and news releases to *School Library Journal* News, 245 W. 17th St., New York, NY 10011. Other journals dedicated to school libraries might also be interested in your program.

Articles. Once you have written and won a grant and are preparing to implement it, you will have an article in your head, just waiting to be written. If you plan from the very beginning of the process to write an article, you can do several things at the outset to get ready to publish.

- Keep notes,
- Take pictures,
- Save clippings, and
- Keep a journal.

Writing an article about the project at its conclusion is a powerful way to disseminate information. Keep good records from the outset; they'll help you write a better article later.

In Your Region and Beyond

Project Fact Sheet. Develop a one-page fact sheet about your project. Have it available to give when you have inquiries about your project.

Brochures. Expand your fact sheet to a brochure. Office supply stores have special brochure paper that can make your publication look professional.

Make a header or footer in your word-processing software crediting the granting organization, and insert it each time you send out a publication.

Once the Project Is Underway

The positive publicity about your grant must continue throughout the life of the grant. The initial press conference and press release may be great, but the work of communicating about your project must continue.

There are two things you have to share: the method you used to write your winning grant and the impact the grant project has had on your school. People interested in school improvement will be interested in hearing about these accomplishments. In a rising tide, all boats rise. What goes around comes around. When you help your colleagues and neighbors help students, good things will come back to you.

Also, your benefactor has a vested interest in your letting others know about the impact of your grant. One of your civic responsibilities when you receive a grant is to make sure that you provide help and information to people who want to know how to replicate your project. That effort is owed to the grantor.

How can you get the word out about the plan you developed and help others reproduce the effects in other locations? There are several ways.

Volunteer

Volunteer to help if you know a team who is writing a grant. Be willing to help proofread their grant or to check the budget figures if that is what they need. Share the names of people at the state department of education who helped you. Volunteer to serve on the writing team when your school applies for a national award.

Presenting

As your project progresses, consider writing a proposal to make a presentation about it at a conference such as one by the American Association of School Librarians (AASL). Presenting at a conference is a terrific way to showcase your library's accomplishments and your benefactor's mission.

Plan a PowerPoint® presentation on how you put your grant project together. Offer to share it at a local or state library conference or for staff development in your school district or diocesan schools. Once you have written proposals and received a grant or two, you have some ideas about applying and getting them. This is knowledge others would like to have. Consider sharing at the national AASL conference or at your local, state, or regional school librarians' conference.

Teach a Class

"Each one teach one" is the rule. When you feel confident you have mastered the art of grant writing and you have information you would like to share with others, consider teaching a class. Successful grant writing is a complex process. Many educators are anxious to learn more about tapping resources for their classes and schools. Sharing that process with others by teaching a class in your school or school district, your region, or at a local community college or university could fulfill a need in your area. Eventually planning to teach a grant writing class is another reason to keep careful notes as you write and receive grants.

You, your students, and your school were fortunate to have received a grant. Now you must share your good fortune with others in a widening circle.

In Your School System, others will want to know about your project and how to reproduce it in their buildings. Volunteer to present your multimedia presentation at district in-service sessions, back-to-school orientation sessions for other librarians, or at a school board meeting. Be sure that you temper your offers to share with grace and humility—two qualities that take us a long way on the road to success.

In the Local Community, your school site council will want to see your multimedia presentation about your project. So might the downtown development council, the Lion's Club, the Rotary, the Parent Teacher Association, the National Education Association leadership team, and many other groups.

In Your State, there are many opportunities for you to volunteer to share your project. The slick multimedia presentation you have developed would make an excellent session at your state school librarian's spring conference. Your former professors at library school might appreciate your sharing the presentation with their current MLS students.

In Your Region. If you collaborated with the social studies teacher to write your grant and develop your project, volunteer to present together with the social studies teacher at the regional conference for teachers of social studies.

Nationally. Volunteer to share your project at the fall conference of school librarians. You could make a difference in the lives of many students by volunteering to share your project with others across the country. Write and submit articles about your project to a variety of school library journals and to online journal publishers.

Internationally. Did you collaborate with the building reading teacher to write your grant? If so, volunteer to present it at the International Reading Association conference or at an international conference of school librarians. Share your project online on your library Web page and on listservs when requested.

Take Stock

What an accomplishment you have achieved! Stop and take time to reflect:

- Have you made a plan to publicize your project in a manner that will be beneficial to both the grantor and to your project?
- Have you thanked and honored your benefactor as well as your team members?
- Have you volunteered to help others?
- Have you shared the project with others in a variety of forums and venues?

Chapter *10*

Follow Through

As long as you are trying your very best, there can be no question of failure.

— Mahatma Gandhi

I t is critical that you follow through, once you receive your grant. You may find that you are required to sign and return a special letter, grant contract, or agreement. Or the grantor may require that your principal or superintendent of schools sign the letter or contract. Read that agreement carefully and make copies of it for your principal, the school system's business office, and any collaborating institutions with which you may be working.

Make note in your calendar system of important due dates, report dates, and other critical information.

One important reason to carefully follow through on your project is that you may want to ask your benefactor to renew the grant or to fund another project sometime in the future. Another reason to do your very best to meet all your commitments is that you are establishing your reputation—and few things are more valuable. Find out right away what the grantor requires of you.

Getting Started

Begin by carefully rereading your original proposal. Make a list of things to be done. Next, contact all the people who will be involved with the project and schedule a meeting to review the scope of the project, the budget, and the timeline.

If there is equipment to be ordered, get started. Keep your evaluation activities in mind so that you get the necessary technology ordered and the students involved as quickly as possible.

Keep Records

At some point, a final report will be due. You will need to keep excellent documentation to be ready to write that report. When it is time to disseminate the results of your project, you will need accurate data. Start now to keep impeccably accurate records and statistics so you'll have exactly the data you need. It is easy to record information and statistics as the project events occur. It is a nightmare to try to reconstruct the data later if you forgot to record it at the time of the event. There is no problem if at the end of the project you have more data than you need. The reverse, however, is not true. If any pretesting is required, be sure it is accomplished and the data recorded.

Budget

How will you receive the funds from your sponsor? Will they go directly into an account at the district business office? Will you need to establish a special account for these funds?

The moment you receive word that your proposal has been funded, set up a method of bookkeeping to keep track of income and expenditures. As you begin to spend money, save the receipts. In order to keep track of your grant funds and expenditures, make a spreadsheet or utilize some other method. The choice of accounting system is yours, but don't delay in setting one up.

Seek assistance immediately upon receipt of the grant to make sure you are managing the funding in a legal manner and according to school, district, and state policy and law. It is exciting to receive your first check, but you must be fiscally responsible.

Reporting

Whether your grant proposal was a formal government regulation grant or an informal letter to a corporate sponsor, you will need to produce a report for your grantor. There are benefits to giving the grantor interim reports, as well, whether or not they are required. Interim reports help you:

- See the progress you are making,

- Keep you focused and on track,
- Keep you on schedule, and
- Help you keep track of loose ends.

An interim report might be as simple as a phone call to your funding organization's program manager. If you have to change an activity in your project, call the grantor and let her know.

Final Report

Your project will probably require a final report. The grantor may give you specific guidelines for the final report, or you may be on your own in designing it. Seek help and advice if you have questions.

Find out to whom the report should be addressed and where it should be sent. Determine if there is a specific due date for the report and what documents should be sent with it.

If for any reason you are going to be late with your report or if you have to make budget changes during the project, be sure to alert the grantor. If your evaluation component is delayed for some reason (maybe the test answer sheet-scanning equipment broke down), call the grantor's program manager and discuss it. If you anticipate a delay, give an estimated new date that you'll furnish the data.

Oversight Committee

One option you may wish to consider is to form an oversight committee to help you oversee the implementation of the grant. Depending on the size of your grant and the complexity of the project, an oversight committee of colleagues who are interested in the project and willing to assist can be invaluable.

Build a Relationship

Establish and maintain a meaningful relationship with your benefactor. Do your best to meet your commitments and execute the plan for which you have been funded. Your benefactor is your ally. Give him your total concentration and effort.

Send newspaper clippings about your project with a note to the grantor. Send him copies of your school newsletter with articles about the project. Drop the

benefactor a note or e-mail if you are selected to make a presentation about the project at a state conference. Keep him in the communication loop. Make sure your Web page is current on the status of the project and that your grantor has the URL.

If your project involves special events or if you are honoring project volunteers with a special reception, invite the grantor.

Site Visit

Does your grant provide for the grant maker to make a site visit? Do you know when that visit will take place? Who from the granting organization will make the visit? Will an auditor be part of the visitor's team and if so, what will she need to see? These are all questions to which you need answers, once you've been told you have the grant.

The site visitors may want to see evidence of:

- Good stewardship of the grant funds,
- Expenditure records,
- Compliance with rules and regulations,
- Adherence to evaluation procedures,
- Completion of activities,
- Student progress, and
- Installation and use of equipment purchased with grant funds.

Evaluation

Most grants include some form of evaluation. After you know the terms of the grant, review your commitment to the evaluation procedure. What have you obligated yourself to do? Do you need to collect comments from students, staff, or patrons as a part of formal evaluation? If so, you will need a notebook or a computer file in which to record the comments that you receive. Could you record video clips or sound recordings of these comments?

Evaluate your project carefully and learn from the process. In addition to collecting data for your formal evaluation report, you may want to informally start collecting video or audio quotes from the students, staff, and parents served by the grant. You could use those comments later for feedback to your benefactor, for inclusion in articles and presentations, and possibly in an interim or final report.

You will need a still (digital) or video camera to record images of special events and of your project in action. If you have received funding for some type of construction, be sure to take "before," "during," and "after" shots of the project: when the bulldozers raze the old facility, at the ground-breaking ceremony for the new digs, and when the new facility opens.

After the Project

Continue to maintain your relationship with your benefactor. Remind yourself to send an occasional note or clipping to keep in touch and let the funding organization know that the project continues to make an impact.

Extensions

Is it possible to reapply for an additional year of funding for your grant? Many grants are issued for one year but offer the opportunity to apply for an additional year of funding. Call your grantor and inquire so that you can decide early in the project whether you will be reapplying. It is sometimes easier to get an additional year of funding for your project than it was to get the initial funding.

After regrouping and gathering up your strength, it may be time to start writing a grant for a new project. Take a little time to savor the good feeling of achieving a really difficult goal—writing a winning grant and, in turn, making improvements for your students. Then pop open that journal of good ideas and let your imagination help you choose your next project.

In summary, the experience of writing a grant proposal, having it selected for funding, and implementing it is enervating, invigorating, exciting hard work. The more positive experience you have with winning grant proposals, the more motivated you will be to write more. May the thrill of grant-writing stay fresh for you, and may you succeed in making your school library media center the student-centered, technology-rich learning environment that you picture in your mind. Most of all, may your students' achievement soar.

Appendix A

Selected Works on Grants and Funding

Articles

Abshire, Sheryl. "Grant Writing Made Easy: Tech Grants Are Widely Available, so Get to a Keyboard and Start Applying. (School Librarian's Toolkit)." *School Library Journal* 48.2 (2002): 38(3).

Anastasi, Valerie, and Mark Hughes. "Grants and Grant Writing." *Phi Delta Kappan* 85.2 (2003): 174.

Anderson, Cynthia. "Write a Grant Today." *Library Media Connection.* Jan. 2003: 44.

Baxter, Veanna. "Library Media Advocacy through Grant Writing." *School Library Media Activities Monthly* 24.2 (2007): 45-47.

Brooks, Douglas. "How to Write GRANTS: The Best Kept Secret in the School Business." *T.H.E. Journal* 31.10 (2004): 30-34.

Brooks-Young, Susan. "Your Wish Is Granted." *School Library Journal* 53.7 (2007): 36-39.

Comolli, Tim. "Going After Grants." *Electronic School* Jan. 2001: 32-34.

Kerney, Carol A. "INSIDE the MIND of a GRANT READER." *Technology & Learning* 25.11 (2005): 62-66.

Knight, Dawn Ventress, and Emma Bradford Perry. "Grant Resources on the Web: Where to Look When You Need Funding." *College and Research Libraries News* 60.7 (1999): 543-545. [Last revised: January 25, 2007]

Mardis, Marcia A. "The Improving Literacy Through School Libraries Program of No Child Left Behind: Tips For Writing a Winning Grant Proposal." *Teacher Librarian* 32.4 (2005): 38-40.

Maxwell, Jackson D. "Money, Money, Money: Taking the pain out of Grant Writing." *Teacher Librarian.* Feb 2005: 16.

McGowan, Judith. "Winning the Grant Game." *School Library Journal* 49.3 (2003): 52.

Nutt, Pam. "Free Cash Giveaway: A Can't Miss Guide to Writing Winning Grants." *School Library Journal* 51.2 (2005): 42.

Pierce, Dennis. "Eight Dos and Don'ts when Seeking Tech Grants." *eschoolnews* (Sept. 1, 2007).

Reese, Susan. "Grant Writing 101." *Techniques: Connecting Education & Careers* 80.4 (2005): 24-27.

Schuckman, Penny. "Grant Writing: Money for the Plucking." *School Administrator* 64.9 (2007): 55-55.

Solomon, Gwen. "Get that Grant: Before and After Pointers." *Technology & Learning* 22.11 (2002): 50.

Tahouri, Parisi. "Winning Grants." *Library Media Connection* (2005) 46-47.

Books

Annual Register of Grant Support 2007, 40th Edition. Medford, NJ: Information Today Inc., 2007.

Bauer, David G. *The "How To" Grants Manual: Successful Grantseeking Techniques for Obtaining Public and Private Grants.* 6th ed. Portsmouth, NH: Greenwood, 2007.

The Big Book of Library Grant Money 2007: Profiles of Private and Corporate Foundations and Direct Corporate Givers Receptive to Library Grand Proposals. Chicago: Information Today, Inc. for American Library Association, 2007.

Browning, Beverly A. *Grant Writing for Dummies*. 2nd ed.. Hoboken, NJ: Wiley Publishing, Inc., 2005.

—. *Grant Writing for Educators: Practical Strategies for Teachers, Administrators, and Staff*. Bloomington, IN: Solution Tree, 2004.

Jacobs, David, ed. *The Foundation Directory, 2006 Edition*. New York: Foundation Center, 2007.

Gajda, Rebecca, and Richard Tulikangas. *Getting the Grant: How Educators Can Write Winning Proposals and Manage Successful Projects*. Alexandria, VA: Association for Supervision and Curriculum Development, 2005.

Geever, Jane C. *Foundation Center's Guide to Proposal Writing*. 5th ed. New York: Foundation Center, 2007.

Gerding, Stephanie K., and Pamela H. MacKellar. *Grants for Libraries: A How-To-Do-It Manual and CD-ROM for Librarians*. New York: Neal-Schuman Publishers Inc., 2006.

Gerin, William. *Writing the NIH Grant Proposal: A Step-by-Step Guide*. Thousand Oaks, CA: Sage Publications, 2006.

Grant$ for Libraries and Information Services 2005-2006. New York: Foundation Center, 2005.

Hall-Ellis, Sylvia D., and Ann Jerabek. *Grants for School Libraries*. Westport, CT: Libraries Unlimited, Inc., 2003.

Hall, Mary S., and Susan Howlett. *Getting Funded: The Complete Guide To Writing Grant Proposals*. 4th ed. Portland, OR: Continuing Education Press, 2003.

Harris, Dianne. *The Complete Guide to Writing Effective & Award-Winning Grants: Step-by-Step Instructions With Companion CD-ROM*. Ocala, FL: Atlantic Publishing Company, 2007.

Hollis, Anthony. *Everything You Need to Know About Grants: How to Write the Grant—How to Get the Grant—Where to Get the Grant*. Lincoln, NE: iUniverse, Inc. 2004.

Jacobs, David, ed. *The Foundation Directory, 2006 Edition*. New York: Foundation Center, 2006.

Karsh, Ellen, and Arlen Sue Fox. *The Only Grant-Writing Book You'll Ever Need: Top Grant Writers and Grant Givers Share Their Secrets*. 2nd ed. New York: Carroll and Graf, 2006.

Miner , Jeremy T. , and Lynn E. Miner. *Models of Proposal Planning & Writing*. Westport, CT: Praeger Publishers, 2005.

Quick, James Aaron, and Cheryl Carter New. *How to Write a Grant Proposal (Wiley Nonprofit Law, Finance and Management Series)*. Hoboken, NJ: John Wiley and Sons, Inc., 2003.

Robinson, Andy. *Grassroots Grants: An Activist's Guide to Grantseeking*. 2nd ed. San Francisco: Jossey-Bass, 2004.

Smith, Nancy Burke, and E. Gabriel Works. *The Complete Book of Grant Writing: Learn to Write Grants like a Professional*. Naperville, IL: Sourcebooks, Inc., 2006.

Thompson, Waddy. *The Complete Idiot's Guide to Grantwriting*. 2nd ed. New York: Penguin Group, Inc., 2007.

Tremore, Judy, and Nancy Burke Smith. *The Everything Grant Writing Book: Create the Perfect Proposal to Raise the Funds You Need*. Avon, MA: Adams Media Corporation, 2003.

Ward, Deborah. *Writing Grant Proposals That Win*. 3rd ed. Boston: Jones and Bartlett, 2006.

Wason, Sara D. *Webster's New World Grant Writing Handbook*. Hoboken, NJ: Wiley, 2004.

Weisblat, Gina. *Get that Grant: Your Guide to Planning Successful K-12 Grant Proposals*. Palm Beach Gardens, FL: LRP Publications, 2006.

Wells, Michael K. *Grantwriting Beyond the Basics: Proven Strategies Professionals Use to Make Their Proposals Work, Book I*. Portland, OR: Continuing Education Press, 2005.

Yang, Otto O. *Guide to Effective Grant Writing: How to Write a Successful NIH Grant Application*. New York: Kluwer Academic/Plenum Publishers, 2005.

Journals and Magazines

Cable in the Classroom. 25 Massachusetts Ave. NW, Suite 100, Washington, DC 20001. 202.222.2335 . <http://www.ciconline.org/cicmagazine>

The Chronicle of Philanthropy. Chronicle of Philanthropy, 1225 23rd St., NW, Washington, DC 20037. <http://www.philanthropy.com/>

Corporate Philanthropy Report. Capitol Publications, 1101 King St., Suite 444, Alexandria, VA 22314.

District Administration. Professional Media Group, LLC, 488 Main Ave., Norwalk, CT 06851. <http://www.districtadministration.com/>

Education Grants Alert. LRP Publications, Palm Beach Gardens, FL, 33418.

Educational Technology. Educational Technology Publications, 700 Palisade Ave., Englewood Cliffs, NJ 07632-0564. 800.952.2665.

Electronic School. <http://www.electronic-school.com.>

eSchool News. eSchool News Communications Group, 7920 Norfolk Ave., Suite 900, Bethesda, MD 20814. 800.394.0115.

Eschool News online. <http://www.eschoolnews.com/>

From Now On: The Educational Technology Journal. <www.fno.org>

Foundation Giving Watch. Taft Group, 27500 Drake Rd., Farmington Hills, MI 48331.

Foundation News & Commentary. Council on Foundations, 1828 L St. NW, Suite 300, Washington, DC 20036.

Learning and Leading with Technology. International Society for Technology in Education, 480 Charnelton St, Eugene, OR 97401-2626. 800.336.5191.

ISTE's Learning & Leading With Technology. <www.iste.org>

Library Media Connection. Linworth Publishing, Inc., 3650 Olentangy River Rd., Suite 250 Columbus, OH 43214. <http://www.linworth.com/lmc/>

Media & Methods Magazine. Media & Methods Magazine, 1429 Walnut St., Philadelphia, PA 19102. <www.media-methods.com>

TechTrends: Linking Research & Practice to Improve Learning. Springer, Neth. <http://www.springerlink.com/home/main.mpx>

Technology and Learning. CMP Media, 600 Community Dr., Manhasset, NY 11030. *TechLearning*. <http://www.techlearning.com/>

T.H.E. Journal. T.H.E. Journal L.L.C., 16261 Laguna Canyon Rd., Suite 130, Irvine, CA 92618. 949-265-1520. <http://thejournal.com/>

Web sites
Government Links
Catalog of Federal Domestic Assistance. <http://www.cfda.gov>

Cooperative State Research, Education, and Extension Service of USDA (CSREES). <http://www.csrees.usda.gov/nea/education/education.html>

Edsitement. <http://edsitement.neh.gov/professional_opportunities.asp>

Grants.gov. <http://www.grants.gov/index.jsp>

Institute of Museum and Library Services. <http://www.imls.gov/applicants/applicants.shtm>

LTP (Learning Technologies Project–NASA). <http://learn.arc.nasa.gov/grants/grants.html>

National Endowment for the Arts. <http://arts.endow.gov/>

National Endowment for the Humanities. <http://www.neh.gov/GRANTS/index.html>
National Science Foundation.
<http://www.nsf.gov/funding/research_edu_community.jsp>
National Telecommunications and Information Administration.
        < http://www.ntia.doc.gov/otiahome/otiahome.html>
U.S. Department of Education. <http://www.ed.gov/>
—, Documents. <http://www.ed.gov/legislation/FedRegister/announcements/index.html>
 —, Electronic Federal Grant Applications. <http://e-grants.ed.gov/egWelcome.asp>
—, Federal Grants Forecast. <http://www.ed.gov/fund/grant/find/edlite-forecast.html>
—, FY 2006-2007 Discretionary Grant Application Packages.
        <http://www.ed.gov/GrantApps/>
—, Funding. <http://www.ed.gov/funding.html>
—, Office of Postsecondary Education, Higher Education Programs.
        <http://www.ed.gov/about/offices/list/ope/index.html>
—, Improving Literacy Through School Libraries.
        <http://www.ed.gov/programs/lsl/index.html>
—, Preparing Tomorrow's Teachers to Use Technology. <http://www.ed.gov/teachtech>
—, 21st Century Community Learning Centers.
        <http://www.ed.gov/programs/21stcclc/index.html>
U.S. Department of Health and Human Services. <http://www.hhs.gov/grantsnet/>

Private Sector
AT&T Foundation. <http://www.att.com/gen/corporate-citizenship?pid=7736>
Annenberg Foundation. <http://www.annenbergfoundation.org/grants/>
Ben & Jerry's Foundation. <http://www.benjerry.com/foundation/>
Benton Foundation. <http://www.benton.org/>
Best Buy Teach Awards. <http://communications.bestbuy.com/communityrelations/teach.asp>
Bill & Melinda Gates Foundation–U.S. Libraries.
        <http://www.gatesfoundation.org/UnitedStates/USLibraryProgram/default.htm>
Brinker International Charitable Committee.
        <http://www.brinker.com/company/givingback.asp>
Broad Foundation. <http://www.broadfoundation.org/home.html>
Carnegie Corporation of New York. <http://www.carnegie.org/>
Coca-Cola Foundation Grants.
        <http://www.thecoca-colacompany.com/citizenship/foundation.html>
Corning Incorporated Foundation Grants.
        <http://www.corning.com/inside_corning/our_commitment/community.aspx>
Dana Foundation. <http://www.dana.org/grants/>
Dow Chemical Company Foundation Grants.
        <http://www.dow.com/about/corp/social/social.htm>
Ewing Marion Kaufmann Foundation. <http://www.kauffman.org/grants.cfm>
Ford Foundation. <http://www.fordfound.org/>
GE Foundation. <http://www.ge.com/foundation/index.html>
GaleSchools.com. <http://www.galeschools.com/grant_goldmine/>
George Lucas Educational Foundation. <http://glef.org/>
Getty Foundation Grants. <http://www.getty.edu/grants/>
Hasbro Children's Fund. <http://www.hasbro.org/default.cfm?page=grantmaking>
Inspiration Software. <http://www.inspiration.com/prodev/index.cfm?fuseaction=scholarship>

Intel in Your Community Grants. <http://www.intel.com/community/grant.htm>
The John D. and Catherine T. MacArthur Foundation.
     <http://www.macfound.org/site/c.lkLXJ8MQKrH/b.3599935/>
Michael Jordan Fundamentals Education Grants Program for Teachers, National Foundation
     for the Improvement of Education. <http://www.jordanfundamentals.com>
Microsoft U.S. Partners in Learning. <http://www.microsoft.com/education/pilus.mspx>
Milken Family Foundation.<http://www.mff.org/initiatives/initiatives.taf>
Pasco. <http://www.pasco.com/resources/funding/GoingForGrants.pdf>
Rockefeller Foundation. <http://www.rockfound.org/>
Sprint Foundation Grants. <http://www.sprint.com/sponsorships/proposalfeedback/
     index.html?id8=vanity:proposals>
Staples Foundation for Learning Grants.
     <http://www.staplesfoundation.org/foundapplication.html>
Starbucks Foundation Grants. <http://www.starbucks.com/aboutus/grantinfo.asp>
State Farm K-12 Public Schools Foundation Grants.
     <http://www.statefarm.com/about/part_spos/community/ed_excel/ed_excel.asp>
Target Educational Grants.
     <http://sites.target.com/site/en/corporate/page.jsp?contentId=PRD03-001838>
Texas Instruments Foundation Grants.
     <http://www.ti.com/corp/docs/company/citizen/education/>
Toshiba America Foundation.
     <http://www.toshiba.com/csrpub/jsp/home/Education.jsp>
Usborne Literacy for a Lifetime Matching Grants.
     <http://www.literacyforalifetime.com/>
W.K. Kellogg Foundation. <http://www.wkkf.org/Default.aspx?LanguageID=0>
Wal-Mart Foundation. <http://walmartstores.com/CommunityGiving/203.aspx>
3M K-12 Education Giving. <http://solutions.3m.com/wps/portal/3M/en_US/
     CommunityAffairs/CommunityGiving/US/K12/>

Organizations & Associations
ALA. <http://www.ala.org/ala/news/libraryfunding/libraryfunding.cfm>
ALA Public Programs Office. <http://www.ala.org/Template.cfm?Section=ppo>
American Association of School Librarians. Resource Guides for School Library Media
     Program Development. <http://www.ala.org/aasl/resources/funding.html>
Association of Fundraising Professionals. <http://www.afpnet.org>
Captain Planet Foundation Grants. <http://www.captainplanetfdn.org/grants.html>
Classroom Connection. <http://www.classroomconnection.org/>
Council for Advancement and Support of Education. <http://www.case.org/>
Council on Foundations. <http://www.cof.org/>
Foundation Center. <http://fdncenter.org/>
Foundations On-line. <http://www.foundations.org>
Fulbright Scholar Program. <http://www.cies.org/us_scholars/>
Fund for Teachers.org. <http://www.fundforteachers.org/about.html>
Grantmakers for Education. <http://www.edfunders.org/>
GrantsWeb. <http://www.srainternational.org/sra03/grantsweb/index.cfm>
Internet Nonprofit Center. <http://nonprofits.org>
Laura Bush Foundation for America's Libraries. <http://www.laurabushfoundation.org>
National Council for the Social Studies. <http://www.ncss.org/>

National Education Association Innovation Grants and Learning & Leadership Grants.
    <http://www.neafoundation.org//grants.htm>
Nonprofit Management Solutions. <http://www.npsolutions.org/resources/resources.asp>
Philanthropy News Digest. <http://foundationcenter.org/pnd/>
Philanthropy News Network Online. <http://pnnonline.org/>
Resource Pages for Educational Grantseekers.
    <http://www.col-ed.org/Funding/funding.html>
SchoolGrants. <http://www.schoolgrants.org>
Schools and Libraries Division of USAC. <http://www.sl.universalservice.org>
The Teachers Network. <www.teachnet.org >

Education Grant Alert Sites (Consolidators)
Education World© Grants for Educators Program.
    <http://www.educationworld.com/a_admin/archives/grants.shtml>
Educational Renaissance Grant Information. <http://www.anovember.com/grants.html>
Grants Alert.com <http://www.grantsalert.com/grants.cfm?id=4&gid=7372>
Grants & Funding for School Technology. <http://www.eschoolnews.com/gf>
Grantsmanship Center. <http://www.tgci.com/>
Internet Library for Librarians: Library Grants. <http://www.itcompany.com/
    inforetriever/grant.htm>
Kathy Schrock's Guide for Educators.
    <http://school.discovery.com/schrockguide/business/grants.html>
Library Support Staff: Fundraising for Libraries Links and Resources.
    <http://www.librarysupportstaff.com/find$.html>
National Center for Public & Private School Foundations.
    <http://www.intime.uni.edu/foundationsk12nc/resources/library.html>
School Funding Center.
    <http://www.schoolfundingcenter.info/(ryulkwao5f51wua33irkmc45)/
    index.aspx>
Teacher Universe. <http://www.riverdeep.net/teacheruniverse/>
Tech.LEARNING Grants & Contests.
    <http://www.techlearning.com/resources/grants.php>

Grant Writing Help
Catalog of Federal Domestic Assistance–Developing and Writing Grant Proposals.
    <http://12.46.245.173/pls/portal30/CATALOG.GRANT_PROPOSAL_DYN.show>
Corporation for Public Broadcasting. <http://www.cpb.org/grants/grantwriting.html>
EPA Grant-Writing Tutorial. <http://www.epa.gov/ogd/recipient/tips.htm>
The Foundation Center's Online Library. <http://fdncenter.org/onlib/index.html>
Grant Proposal Writing. <http://www.wilbers.com/grants.htm>
Grantwriters.com. <www.grantwriters.com>
Hooked on Grantwriting: A WebQuest for Adults.
    <http://www.kathydoty.addr.com/wq/t-index.htm>
Scholastic. <http://content.scholastic.com/browse/article.jsp?id=4173>
School Grants. Tips on grant writing. <http://schoolgrants.org/tips>
TGCI (The Grantsmanship Center). <http://www.tgci.com>

Appendix B

U.S. Department of Education Technology Programs

Guide to U.S. Department of Education Programs 2007
> <http://www.ed.gov/programs/gtep/gtep.pdf>

Enhancing Education Through Technology Program

The primary goal of this program is to improve student achievement through the use of technology in elementary and secondary schools. An additional goal is to help all students become technologically literate by the end of the 8th grade.
<http://www.ed.gov/programs/edtech/index.html>.

Technical Assistance

The *Regional Technology in Education Consortia*'s six centers provide states, school districts, adult literacy programs, and other education institutions with professional development, technical assistance, and information about the use of advanced technologies to improve teaching and learning. 202.219.8070 or <http://rtec.org/>.

Other Federal Resources

The Federal Communications Commission oversees the E-Rate (Education Rate), which provides affordable access to advanced telecommunications services for all schools and libraries in the United States. Contact the Schools and Libraries Division at 888.203.8100 or go to <http://www.sl.universalservice.org/>.

The National Science Foundation makes grants and awards in all areas of science, mathematics, and engineering education. Contact NSF at 703.292.5111 or go to <http://www.nsf.gov/funding/research_edu_community.jsp>.

The Department of Energy's 10 national laboratories and 30 technology centers and research facilities provide educational experiences for students, training and curriculum materials for preservice and inservice teachers, and literacy programs for the general public. DOE also runs Computers for Learning, which will place hundreds of thousands of surplus government computers in U.S. classrooms. Contact Computers for Learning at 866.472-9161 or go to <http://www.computers.fed.gov>.

National Aeronautics and Space Administration (NASA) provides online educational programs and services. Visit <http://www.education.nasa.gov>.

The U.S. Department of Agriculture's Distance Learning and Telemedicine grants support telemedicine services and distance learning services in rural areas. Contact the Rural Utilities Service at 202.720.0413 or go to <http://www.usda.gov/rus/telecom/dlt/dlt.htm>.

The U.S. Department of Education's Office of Educational Technology (OET) develops national educational technology policy and coordinates and implements this policy through its programs. Working closely with the offices of Elementary and Secondary

Education (OESE), Educational Research and Improvement (OERI), Postsecondary Education (OPE), Vocational and Adult Education (OVAE), and Special Education and Rehabilitative Services (OSERS), OET helps to ensure that these programs are also coordinated with efforts across the federal government. A primary focus of OET's work is evaluating the effectiveness of educational technology. OET's leadership priorities currently include:

- Promoting equal access to technology,
- Ensuring Internet safety,
- Encouraging new strategies for software development, and
- Planning the nation's long-term policy for educational technology.

Educational Technology publications are available at
<http://www.ed.gov/about/offices/list/os/technology/index.html>
or by calling 877.4ED.PUBS or 877.576.7734.

The top five publications are:

- *No Child Left Behind Empowering Parents School Box*
- *Shining Stars: Toddlers Get Ready To Read: How Parents Can Help Their Toddlers Get Ready To Read*
- *Shining Stars: Preschoolers Get Ready To Read: How Parents Can Help Their Preschoolers Get Ready To Read*
- *A Child Becomes A Reader: Proven Ideas From Research For Parents: Birth Through Preschool*
- *Shining Stars: Kindergartners Learn How To Read: How Parents Can Help Their Kindergartners Learn to Read*

National Education Technology Plan

In 2005 OET produced the publication *The National Education Technology Plan*, which provides a summary of the challenges in our schools, the importance of technology, current student attitudes regarding technology, and recommendations for meeting the challenges of No Child Left Behind through technology.

Action Steps

To help states and districts prepare today's students for the opportunities and challenges of tomorrow, a set of seven action steps and accompanying recommendations have been developed:

1. Strengthen Leadership
2. Consider Innovative Budgeting
3. Improve Teacher Training
4. Support E-Learning and Virtual Schools
5. Encourage Broadband Access
6. Move Toward Digital Content
7. Integrate Data Systems

For more information about each of these action steps go to
<http://www.ed.gov/about/offices/list/os/technology/plan/2004/site/edlite-default.html>

Appendix C

Glossary

Abstract. A cogent summary of a proposed project; a quick overview, usually one page, used to persuade the reader to read the proposal and the grantor to fund it.

Acronyms. Words formed by the initial letters of a name or series of words. Example: ED is Education Department.

Activities. Events planned to accomplish the goals of a project.

Analog. A system that relies on computer-based reproduction of sound and image.

Annual report. An account of the achievements and financial information of an organization for the past year, which usually includes a sponsor's goals and mission.

Appendices. Attachments to a grant proposal. They may include resumes, organizational charts, agency publications, letters of support, reprints of articles, other supporting data.

Applicant. Person or organization seeking grant funding.

Application notice. A government notice published in the *Federal Register* that invites applications for one or more discretionary grant or cooperative agreement competitions, gives basic program and fiscal information on each competition, informs potential applicants of when and where they can obtain applications, and cites the deadline for applying.*

Application package. Package containing the application notice for one or more programs and all the information and forms needed to apply for a discretionary grant.*

Appropriations legislation. A law passed by Congress to provide a certain level of funding for a grant program in a given year.*

Authorizing agent. The person appointed by the school board to sign legal documents.

Authorizing legislation. A law passed by Congress that establishes or continues a grant program.*

Award. A grant.

Award notice. Formal notification from grantor to applicant announcing award of a grant.

Baseline data. Evaluation data demonstrating the status prior to implementation of the grant project.

Benchmarks. Interim reference points during a grant project that indicate progress.

Block grant. A type of government grant issued to another unit of government for dispersal determined by a formula.

Blog. Short for "Web log." A specialized Web site that allows an individual or group of individuals to share a running log of events and personal insights with online audiences; a frequently updated online journal or diary. Blog can also be used as a verb, meaning to maintain or add content to a blog. Ex.: "Have you blogged today?"

Budget period. An interval of time into which a project period is divided for budgetary purposes, usually 12 months.*

Capital outlay. Furniture, equipment, and hardware such as computers, tables, and projectors.

Catalog of Federal Domestic Assistance **(CFDA).** Publication and database produced by the General Services Administration that lists the domestic assistance programs of all federal agencies with information about authorization, fiscal details, accomplishments, regulations, guidelines, eligibility requirements, information contacts, and application and award process.*

Coalition. A group of interested parties or organizations who come together for a special purpose.

Competitive review process. The process used by the U.S. Department of Education to evaluate grant proposals and cooperative agreement applications in which applications are scored by subject-area experts and those with highest scores considered for funding.*

Consortium. A group of organizations who join together to submit a grant application.

Construction grant. Money awarded for building or renovating facilities.

Continuation application. A request to continue funding for an existing project for an additional time period.

Continuation grant. Additional funding awarded for budget periods following the initial budget period of a multi-year grant.*

Cost Sharing. Costs that a school or district will contribute to the project. They can be "in-kind" costs such as the use of space or volunteers, as well as actual cash outlay.

Criteria. Characteristics on which a proposal will be evaluated.

curriculum vitae. Resume, brief summary of one's education, professional history, and job qualifications.

Deadline. The date by which an applicant must mail a grant application for it to be considered for funding. In some competitions, the grantor requires that the application be received by the deadline date, not just mailed by that date.*

Demographic data. Statistical or factual information about a target group or community.

Digital. A system that measures physical changes in variable qualities such as sound waves.

Direct assistance. A grant that provides personnel, equipment, or supplies, not money.

Direct costs. Line items explicitly listed in the budget as expenditures.

Discretionary grant. An award of financial assistance in the form of money, or property in lieu of money, by the federal government to an eligible grantee, usually made on the basis of a competitive review process.*

Dissemination. The means by which information is given to others about a project. Usually includes purpose, methods, and accomplishments of the project; may be a section of a grant proposal.

E-Rate. A federal fund to help schools and libraries gain Internet access at a reasonable price.

ED. The acronym for the U.S. Department of Education.*

Employee benefits. Fringe benefits, such as health insurance.

Evaluation. The manner in which a project's impact on students or participants will be measured.

Executive summary. An abstract; the concise description of a project. A section of a grant proposal.

Federal Register. A daily compilation of federal regulations and legal notices, presidential proclamations and executive orders, federal agency documents having general applicability and legal effect, documents required to be published by an act of Congress, and other federal agency documents of public interest; prepared by the National Archives and Records Administration for public distribution by the Government Printing Office; publication of record for ED regulations.*

Fiscal year. A 12-month period for budget purposes.

Formative evaluation. A type of project evaluation designed to provide immediate feedback. It assesses procedures used and progress being made.

Formula grant. A grant that the U.S. Department of Education is directed by Congress to make to grantees, for which the amount is established by a formula based on certain criteria that are written into the legislation and program regulations; directly awarded and administered in the Department of Education's program offices.*

Fringe benefits. Amounts paid by an employer for retirement, health insurance, and other employee benefits.

Full-time equivalent (FTE). A weighted formula that accounts for part-time, special needs, non-English-speaking, and other categories of students in terms of full-time enrollment.

Funding offer. A U.S. Department of Education proposal, either oral or written, that an applicant accept a level of funding less than the applicant's request. This occurs when the Department either does not accept certain items of cost in the applicant's original budget or does not have sufficient money to fund all recommended projects at the requested level.*

Goals. Purpose of a project.

Government grant. Funding from the federal, state, or local government.

Grant. Financial assistance given for a specific purpose and time period as outlined in an application or proposal.

Grant application reviewer (reviewer). An individual who serves the U.S. Department of Education by reviewing new discretionary grant applications; also referred to as 'field reader' or 'peer reviewer.'*

Grant Award Notification (GAN). Official document signed by an authorized official stating the amount, terms, and conditions of an award for a discretionary grant or cooperative agreement from the U.S. Department of Education.*

Grant closeout. The final phase in the life cycle of a discretionary grant during which the U.S. Department of Education ensures that the grantee has met the requirements of a grant and makes final fiscal adjustments to a grantee's account.*

Grantee. The person or group of people receiving a grant.

Grantor. The entity making the grant funds available.

Grants Management Office. Someone on the grantor's staff who oversees dispersal of grant funds.

Guidelines. Rules, regulations, and specifications to be followed in applying for a grant.

Higher Education Programs (HEP). A section of the U.S. Department of Education.

Indirect costs. Costs incurred for common or joint objectives that cannot be readily and specifically identified with a particular grant project or other institutional activity.* Costs not explicitly listed in the budget as a line item. Private foundations usually refer to indirect costs as *administrative costs*. Corporations may call the same costs *overhead*.

In-kind support. Grantee's non-cash contributions to a grant project.

Letter of intent. A letter to a grantor briefly describing a project and requesting permission to apply for a grant.

Letter of support or commitment. A letter from a supervisor, expert, or stakeholder to a grantor vouching for an applicant's credentials and a project's potential success.

Local education agency (LEA). The school district or educational service agency that will receive and disburse the grant funds.

MP3. MP3 is slang for "MPEG Layer-3". MPEG stands for "Moving Picture Experts Group" and refers to the experts who developed MPEG–a set of industry standards for digitally encoding video and audio information. Files can be transferred via the internet and stored in portable players.

Matching funds. Money or in-kind services a grantor requires a recipient to contribute.

Mission. An organization's chief function or responsibility.

Monitoring. Activities undertaken by U.S. Department of Education staff members to review and evaluate specific aspects of a grantee's activities under a discretionary grant; they include:
- Measuring a grantee's performance,
- Assessing a grantee's adherence to applicable laws, regulations, and terms and conditions of the award,
- Providing technical assistance, and
- Assessing whether a grantee has made substantial progress.*

Moodle. A Virtual Professional Learning Community. Moodle stands for **M**odular **O**bject-**O**riented **D**ynamic **L**earning **E**nvironment. Within Moodle teachers can add Web sites, discussion boards, chat rooms, wikis, podcasts, assignments, quizzes and lessons.

Needs statement. The section of the proposal that describes the need for the project. It usually contains meaningful statistics and educational research.

Notice of grant award. The formal notification from the grantor describing the grant amount, requirements and time periods.

Objectives. Measurable statements or outcomes that demonstrate changes or growth resulting from a project.

Oversight committee. An advisory group charged with overseeing the administration of a grant.

Partnership. An alliance formed between individuals or groups in order to participate in a mutually advantageous project.

Performance report. A report of the specific activities the grant recipient has performed during the budget or project period.*

Personal digital assistant (PDA). Hand-held electronic device for computing and data storage and retrieval.

Post-award performance conference. The first major discussion between the U.S. Department of Education and some grantees after a new award has been made, generally focusing on the proposed project outcomes as stated in the grantee's approved application and on the ways in which progress will be assessed.*

Per diem. The cost per day for the travel expenses, hotel, and meals.

Podcast. An audio or video recording posted on a Web site that can be downloaded and played later. Originally derived from a combination of "broadcasting" and "iPod," the word was declared "word of the year" when it was added to the dictionary at the end of 2005.

Program announcement. Notification in the Federal Register describing an opportunity to apply for a grant.

Program officer. The person who supervises grant funds for a philanthropic organization and explains program guidelines and the benefactor's mission to applicants.

Program regulations. Regulations that implement legislation passed by Congress to authorize a specific grant program; they include:
- Applicant and participant eligibility criteria,
- Nature of activities funded,
- Costs allowed,
- Selection criteria, and
- Other relevant information.*

Project officer. See *Program officer* (above).

Project period. The total amount of time (sometimes several years) during which the grantor authorizes a grantee to complete the project described in the application. Project periods of more than one year are divided into budget periods. Sometimes referred to as 'performance period.'*

Proposal. A written document of detailed information about a proposed project that an applicant submits to a grantor.

Proposal letter. A preliminary proposal sent in the form of a letter.

Query Letter. A letter sent to a potential grantor outlining a broad overview of the project proposal. The grantee is exploring the funding source's interest in the project before submitting a formal proposal.

RSS Feed. Really Simple Syndication is a popular technology for notifying users of updates to content in a Web site or blog.

RSS Feed Aggregator. A Web application that aggregates, or brings together, syndicated Web content such as news headlines, blogs, podcasts, and vlogs in a single location for easy viewing.

Request for proposal (RFP) or request for application (RFA). A grantor's request for submissions. Usually includes guidelines and necessary forms.

Rubric. A form, provided by the grantor, used for scoring a grant proposal. The rubric may or may not be included in the guidelines.

Sponsor. The grantor.

Staff development. Continuing education opportunity for staff involved in the grant project.

Stakeholders. The people in an organization who will participate in or benefit from a grant project.

Statement of purpose. A section of the proposal describing the intended results anticipated from the implementation of a project.

Stipend. A payment provided for participation in or service to a project.

Substantial progress. A level of achievement that a grantee must make in its project during a specified period of time (e.g., budget period, performance period), which produces measurable and verifiable evidence that the activities undertaken have attained a preponderance of project goals and objectives during the period.*

Summation evaluation. The final evaluation of a project's results.

Timeline. A graph or narrative explaining which tasks are to be accomplished, by whom, over which time periods.

Unsolicited proposal. A proposal sent without the grantor's request.

Video streaming. A method of delivering motion video with audio live through the Internet. The user does not have to download a file to a computer and then play it back.

Vision. The plan envisioned for the future of a project or organization.

Web 2.0. A term introduced in 2004 referring to the second generation of the Web. An ongoing transition of the World Wide Web from a collection of Web sites to social networking sites, such as wikis and blogs–sites that emphasize online collaboration and sharing among users. It encourages user participation.

Weblog (Blog). An online journal or diary that is frequently updated (also referred to as a blog).

Wiki. A Web site that allows visitors to add remove, edit, and change content. Users are able to easily edit, create, and link Web pages. A collaborative Web site that can be directly edited by anyone with access to it.

*Definitions provided by the U.S. Department of Education publication *What Should I Know About ED Grants?*

Appendix D

Top 10 U.S. Foundations by Total Giving

The list below includes the 10 largest U.S. grant-making foundations ranked by total giving, based on the most current audited financial data in the Foundation Center's database as of June 26, 2008. Total giving figures include grants, scholarships, employee matching gifts, and other amounts reported as "grants and contributions paid during the year" on the 990-PF tax form. Total giving does not include all qualifying distributions under the tax law, e.g., loans, program-related investments, and program or other administrative expenses. Fiscal records will be updated when more recent audited financial information is obtained.

Rank	Name/(state)	Total Giving	As of Fiscal Year End Date
1.	Bill & Melinda Gates Foundation (WA)	$2,011,675,000	12/31/07
2.	The Ford Foundation (NY)	583,915,463	9/30/07
3.	The William and Flora Hewlett Foundation (CA)	421,400,000	12/31/07
4.	The Bristol-Myers Squibb Patient Assistance Foundation, Inc. (NJ)	416,632,202	12/31/06
5.	The Robert Wood Johnson Foundation (NJ)	367,570,000	12/31/06
6.	Lilly Endowment, Inc. (IN)	341,863,979	12/31/07
7.	Janssen Ortho Patient Assistance Foundation, Inc. (NJ)	339,648,095	12/31/06
8.	GlaxoSmithKline Patient Access Programs Foundation (NC)	324,284,214	12/31/06
9.	W. K. Kellogg Foundation (MI)	302,844,012	8/31/07
10.	The Annenberg Foundation (PA)	279,744,155	6/30/07

Source: **Foundation Center**
<http://foundationcenter.org/findfunders/topfunders/top100giving.html>

Appendix E

Sample Grant Proposal Format

(Hypothetical)

Six Pages Maximum

Page 1

Project Cover Page

Page 2

Project Summary

(One page that includes the overview of the project's goals)

Page 3-5

Project Description—give a detailed description of the project and answer the following questions (Maximum–three pages).

$2,000 Level completes steps 1-7 listed below
$4,000 Level completes steps 1-9 listed below

Project Description

1. Demonstrate the need.
2. How will the project be implemented and by whom? (Outline and timeline of activities)
3. How is your grant innovative?
4. How many students will be involved?

Project Description

5. How will you assess the impact on students?
6. How will the project link students to the community and to their own futures?
7. How will the community learn about your project?

Project Description

8. How will the project link school to the workplace and/or integrate academic and technical learning?
9. Explain the role of the community partner.

Page 6

Budget

- An itemized budget of how the money will be spent to support the grant objectives and goals.
- Include any cash donations, time, service, or materials that have been secured.
- If the project will require additional funding beyond the grant, explain how these funds will be raised.

Directory of State Humanities Councils, Spring 2008

Alabama
Alabama Humanities Foundation
1100 Ireland Way, Suite 101
Birmingham, AL 35205-7001
205.558.3980 / 205.558.3981 (fax)
Web:

Alaska
Alaska Humanities Forum
421 West First Avenue, Suite 300
Anchorage, AK 99501
907.272.5341 / 907.272.3979 (fax)
Web:

American Samoa
Amerika Samoa Humanities Council
P.O. Box 5800
Pago Pago, AS 96799
684.633.4870 / 684.633.4873 (fax)
Web: Unavailable

Arizona
Arizona Humanities Council
The Ellis-Shackelford House
1242 North Central Avenue
Phoenix, AZ 85004
602.257.0335 / 602.257.0392 (fax)
Web:

Arkansas
Arkansas Humanities Council
10800 Financial Centre Parkway, Suite 465
Little Rock, AR 72211
501.221.0091 / 501.221.9860 (fax)
Web:

California
California Council for the Humanities
312 Sutter Street, Suite 601
San Francisco, CA 94108
415.391.1474 / 415.391.1312 (fax)
Web:

Colorado
Colorado Endowment for the Humanities
1490 Lafayette Street, Suite 101
Denver, CO 80218
303.894.7951 / 303.864.9361 (fax)
Web: <www.coloradohumanities.org>

Connecticut
Connecticut Humanities Council
95 South Main Street, #E
Middletown, CT 06457
860.685.2260 / 860.685-7597 (fax)
Web: <www.ctculture.org>

Delaware
Delaware Humanities Forum
100 West 10th Street, Suite 1009
Wilmington, DE 19801
302.657.0650 / 302.657.0655 (fax)
Web:

District of Columbia
Humanities Council of Washington, D.C.
925 U Street, NW
Washington, DC 20001
202.387.8393 / 202.387.8149 (fax)
Web: <http://wdchumanities.org/>

Florida
Florida Humanities Council
599 2nd Street S
St. Petersburg, FL 33701-5005
727.873.2000 / 727.873.2014 (fax)
Web:

Georgia
Georgia Humanities Council
50 Hurt Plaza, SE, Suite 595
Atlanta, GA 30303-2915
404.523.6220 / 404.523.5702 (fax)
Web:

Guam
Guam Humanities Council
222 Chalan Santo Papa
Reflection Center, Suite 106
Hagatna, Guam 96910
671.472.4460 / 671.646.2243 (fax)
Web:

Hawaii

Hawaii Council for the Humanities
First Hawaiian Bank Building
3599 Waialae Avenue, Room 23
Honolulu, HI 96816
808.732.5402 / 808.732.5402 (fax)
Web: <www.hihumanities.org>

Idaho

Idaho Humanities Council
217 West State Street
Boise, ID 83702
208.345.5346 / 208.345.5347
Web:

Illinois

Illinois Humanities Council
Suite 1400
17 North State Street
Chicago, IL 60602-3296
312.422.5580 / 312.422.5588 (fax)
Web:

Indiana

Indiana Humanities Council
1500 North Delaware Street
Indianapolis, IN 46202
317.638.1500 / 317.634.9503 (fax)
Web:

Iowa

Humanities Iowa
100 Oakdale Campus, Northlawn
University of Iowa
Iowa City, IA 52242-5000
319.335.4153 / 319.335.4154 (fax)
Web:

Kansas

Kansas Humanities Council
112 SW Sixth Avenue, Suite 210
Topeka, KS 66603
785.357.0359 / 785.357.1723 (fax)
Web: <www.kansashumanities.org>

Kentucky

Kentucky Humanities Council
206 East Maxwell Street
Lexington, KY 40508
859.257.5932 / 859.257.5933 (fax)
Web: <www.kyhumanities.org>

Louisiana

Louisiana Endowment for the Humanities
938 Lafayette Street, Suite 300
New Orleans, LA 70113
504.523.4352 / 504.529.2358 (fax)
Web:

Maine

Maine Humanities Council
674 Brighton Avenue
Portland, ME 04102-1012
207.773.5051 / 207.773.2416 (fax)
Web:

Maryland

Maryland Humanities Council
108 West Centre Street
Baltimore, MD 21201-4565
410.685.0095 / 410.771.0655 (fax)
Web:

Massachusetts

Massachusetts Foundation for the Humanities
66 Bridge Street
Northampton, MA 01060
413.584.8440 / 413.584.8454
Web:

Michigan

Michigan Humanities Council
119 Pere Marquette Drive, Suite 3B
Lansing, MI 48912-1270
517.372.7770 / 517.372.0027 (fax)
Web: <http://michiganhumanities.org>

Minnesota

Minnesota Humanities Center
987 East Ivy Avenue
St. Paul, MN 55106
651.774.0105 / 651.774.0205 (fax)

Mississippi

Mississippi Humanities Council
3825 Ridgewood Road, Room 311
Jackson, MS 39211
601.432.6752 / 601.432.6750 (fax)
Web: <www.mshumanities.org>

Missouri

Missouri Humanities Council
543 Hanley Industrial Court, Suite 201
St. Louis, MO 63144
314.781.9660 / 314.781.9681 (fax)
Web:

Montana

Humanities Montana
311 Brantly Hall
University of Montana
Missoula, MT 59812-8214
406.243.6022 / 406.243.4836 (fax)
Web: <www.umt.edu/lastbest>

Nebraska
Nebraska Humanities Council
Suite 225 Lincoln Center Building
215 Centennial Mall South
Lincoln, NE 68508
402.474.2131 / 402.474.4852 (fax)
Web:

Nevada
Nevada Humanities Committee
1034 N. Sierra Street
Reno, NV 89507
775.784.6587 / 775.784.6527 (fax)
Web: <www.nevadahumanities.org>

New Hampshire
New Hampshire Humanities Council
19 Pillsbury Street
Concord, NH 03301-2228
603.224.4071 / 603.224.4072 (fax)
Web:

New Jersey
New Jersey Council for the Humanities
28 West State Street, 6th Floor
Trenton, NJ 08608
609.695.4838 / 609.695.4929
Web:

New Mexico
New Mexico Humanities Council
MSC06 3570
1 University of New Mexico
Albuquerque, NM 87131-0001
505.277.6156 / 505.277.6056 (fax)
Web:

New York
New York Council for the Humanities
150 Broadway, Suite 1700
New York, NY 10038
212.233.1131 / 212.233.4607 (fax)
Web:

North Carolina

North Carolina Humanities Council
200 South Elm Street, Suite 601
Greensboro, NC 27401
336.334.5325 / 336.334.5052 (fax)
Web:

North Dakota
North Dakota Humanities Council
418 East Broadway, Suite 8
P.O. Box 2191
Bismarck, ND 58502
701.255.3360 / 701.223.8724 (fax)
Web:

Ohio
Ohio Humanities Council
471 E. Broad Street, Suite 1620
Columbus, OH 43215-3857
614.461.7802 / 614.461.4651 (fax)
Web:

Oklahoma
Oklahoma Humanities Council
Festival Plaza
428 West California, Suite 270
Oklahoma City, OK 73102
405.235.0280 / 405.235.0289 (fax)
Web:

Oregon
Oregon Council for the Humanities
812 SW Washington Street, Suite 225
Portland, OR 97205
503.241.0543 / 503.241.0024 (fax)
Web:

Pennsylvania
Pennsylvania Humanities Council
325 Chestnut Street, Suite 715
Philadelphia, PA 19106
215.925.1005 / 215.925.3054 (fax)
Web:

Puerto Rico
Fundación Puertorriqueña de las
Humanidades
109 San Jose Street, 3rd floor
Box 9023920
San Jaun, PR 00902-3920
787.721.2087 / 787.721.2684 (fax)
Web:

Rhode Island

Rhode Island Committee for the Humanities
385 Westminster Street, Suite 2
Providence, RI 02903
401.273.2250 / 401.454.4872 (fax)
Web: <www.rihumanities.org>

South Carolina
The Humanities Council of South Carolina
2711 Middleburg Drive, Suite 308
P.O. Box 5287
Columbia, SC 29254
803.691.4100 / 803.691.0809 (fax)
Web: <www.schumanities.org/>

South Dakota
South Dakota Humanities Council
1215 Trail Ridge Road, Suite A
Brookings, SD 57006
605.688.6113 / 605.688.4531 (fax)
Web: <http://web.sdstate.edu/humanities/ >

Tennessee
Humanities Tennessee
306 Gay Street, Suite 306
Nashville, TN 37201
615.770.0006 / 615.770.0007 (fax)
Web: <www.humanitiestennessee.org>

Texas
Humanities Texas
1410 Rio Grande Street
Austin, Texas 78701
512.440.1991 / 512.440.0115 (fax)
Web: <www.humanitiestexas.org/>

Utah
Utah Humanities Council
202 West 300 North
Salt Lake City, UT 84103-1108
801.359.9670 / 801.531.7869 (fax)
Web: <www.utahhumanities.org/>

Vermont
Vermont Council on the Humanities
11 Loomis Street
Montpelier, VT 05602
802-262-2626 / 802-262-2620 (fax)
Web: <www.vermonthumanities.org/>

Virgin Islands

Virgin Islands Humanities Council
1826 Kongens Gade 5-6, Suite 2
St. Thomas, VI 00802-6746
340.776.4044 / 340.774.3972 (fax)
Web: <www.vihumanities.org>

Virginia
Virginia Foundation for the Humanities and
Public Policy
145 Ednam Drive
Charlottesville, VA 22903-4629
804.924.3296 / 804.296.4714 (fax)
Web: <www.virginia.edu/vfh/>

Washington
Humanities Washington
615 Second Avenue, Suite 300
Seattle, WA 98104
206.682.1770 / 206.682.4158 (fax)
Web: <www.humanities.org/>

West Virginia
West Virginia Humanities Council
1310 Kanawha Blvd. East, Suite 800
Charleston, WV 25301
304.346.8500 / 304.346.8504 (fax)
Web: <www.wvhumanities.org>

Wisconsin
Wisconsin Humanities Council
222 South Bedford Street, Suite F
Madison, WI 53703-3688
608.262.0706 / 608.263.7970 (fax)
Web: <www.wisconsinhumanities.org>

Wyoming
Wyoming Council for the Humanities
1315 E. Lewis Street
Laramie, WY 82072-3459
307.721.9243 / 307.742.4914 (fax)
Web: <www.uwyo.edu/HUMANITIES>

Appendix G

Technology Inventory

Location	Type of Hardware	Manufacturer	Model	Serial Number	Assest Tag	Comment
(Example: Library or Computer Lab)	(Example: CPU, Monitor, Printer)	(Example: IBM, MAC, Compaq)				
Example:						
Library	CPU	Compaq	1234567	88999	X	

Date_____ Librarian_____ School_____

Appendix H

Listservs for School Librarians

AASLFORUM is offered to all personal members of AASL Members Forum. They may also subscribe to the specialized discussion list exclusively for their subsection: Educators of Library Media Specialists Section (ELMSS), Independent Schools Section (ISS), or Supervisors Section (SPVS).

To subscribe to any of these lists, send an e-mail message to *LISTPROC@ala.org*. In the subject line of the message, type **subscribe**. For the first and only line of text in the body of the message type **subscribe listname Your name member #**.

Substitute the name of the list to which you wish to subscribe such as AASLFORUM, ELMSS, ISS or SPVS and your own first and last names. Your request must include your ALA personal member number.

LM_NET is an international listserv for school library media specialists on the Internet. To join, send an e-mail message to *LISTSERV@listserv.syr.edu*. Place nothing in the subject line and the words **subscribe lm_net** and **your own name** in the body of the message.

AASL News, the listserv of the American Association of School Librarians (AASL), is a "read only" listserv open to AASL members and non-members. To subscribe, send an e-mail message to *LISTPROC@ala.org*. Put nothing in the subject line and the words **subscribe aaslnews** and **your own name** in the body of the message.

Bring Home the Bacon is an electronic newsletter sponsored by *SchoolGrants*. To join send a message to *LISTSERV@netpals.lsoft.com*. In the body of the message, type the following commands: **SUBSCRIBE BRINGHOMEBACON YourFirstName YourLastName**.

To subscribe to their monthly newsletter, send a blank e-mail requesting **subscribe@schoolgrants.org**.

BIG6 is a worldwide discussion group is for school library media specialists and other educators interested in the Big 6 Skills approach to information literacy skills instruction. To join, send an e-mail to *LISTSERV@listserv.syr.edu* with nothing in the subject line. Add the words **subscribe Big6** and **your own name** in the body of the message.

BooKBrag, sponsored by the Scholastic Network for teachers and librarians, contains a monthly newsletter, book reviews, author talk, and input from teachers. To subscribe, send an e-mail to *BooKBrag-request@scholastic.com*. Put nothing in the subject line. In the body of the message type the words **subscribe bookbrag** and **your own name**.

CCBC-NET is set by the School of Education, University of Wisconsin-Madison, to encourage the discussion of books for children and young adults. To join, go to the following Web site and enter your personal information: <http://post.education.wisc.edu/mailman/listinfo/ccbc-net>

EDInfo will keep you updated on government grant opportunities. To subscribe, address an e-mail to *LISTSERV@listserv.ed.gov*. Then write **subscribe EDInfo** and **Your own name** in the message.

EDTECH is a listserv for the discussion of all aspects of technology and its use in education. To join, go to the following Web site and enter your personal information: <http://miller.tea.state.tx.us/cgi-bin/wa?SUBED2=name&A=1&L=Edtech&b.x=57&b.y=10>

KIDLIT-L is for you if you are interested in discussing children's literature online. To join, send an e-mail to *LISTSERV@bingvmb.bitnet* placing nothing in the subject line. In the body of the message put the words **subscribe kidlit-l** and **your own name**.

PND-L. Philanthropy News Digest will send you an e-mail version of *Philanthropy News Digest*, the Foundation Center's digest of philanthropy-related news, once a week if you sign up. Send a message to *LISTSERV@lists.foundationcenter.org* with the words **SUBSCRIBE PND-L** and **your name** in the message.

The following states as of January 2007 have state listservs:

Alabama, Arizona, Arkansas, California, Colorado, Connecticut, Delaware, Georgia, Idaho, Illinois, Indiana, Iowa, Kansas, Kentucky, Maine, Massachusetts, Michigan, Minnesota, Missouri, Montana, Nebraska, New Hampshire, New Jersey, New Mexico, New York, North Carolina, North Dakota, Ohio, Oregon, Pennsylvania, Rhode Island, South Carolina, South Dakota, Tennessee, Texas, Utah, Virginia, Washington, Wisconsin.

Check with your state library association if you don't see your state listed.

Appendix I*

Awards and Contests

ALA

Awards
<http://www.ala.org/Template.cfm?Section=awards>

Grants & Fellowships
<http://www.ala.org/Template.cfm?Section=grantfellowship>

YALSA Awards and Grants
<http://www.ala.org/ala/yalsa/awardsandgrants/yalsaawardsgrants.cfm>

AASL Awards, Grants & Scholarships
<http://www.ala.org/aasltemplate.cfm?Section=aaslawards>

Alibris

Alibris Collection Award
<http://www.alibris.com/librarians/collection_award.cfm>

ALISE/Linworth Youth Services Paper Award

<http://www.alise.org/mc/page.do?sitePageId=55541>

Captain Planet

Captain Planet Foundation Grants
<http://www.captainplanetfdn.org/grants.html>

Dollar General

Beyond Words: the Dollar General School Library Relief Fund
<http://www.ala.org/ala/aasl/aaslawards/dollargeneral/disasterrelief.cfm>

DonorsChoose.org

Teachers Ask - You Choose
<http://www.donorschoose.org/homepage/main.html>

Ezra Jack Keats Foundation

Ezra Jack Keats Mini Grants
<http://www.ezra-jack-keats.org/programs/minigrant.html>

Gale

Gale/ LMC TEAMS Award
<http://www.galeschools.com>

H.W. Wilson

John Cotton Dana Library Public Relations Award
<http://www.hwwilson.com/jcdawards/nw_jcd.htm>

IRA (International Reading Association)
Awards and Grants
<http://www.reading.org/association/awards/>

James Patterson
Page Turner Awards
<http://www.pattersonpageturner.org/>

Lilly Endowment
Teacher Creativity Fellowship Grant (Indiana)
<http://www.lillyendowment.org/ed_tc.html>

LITA (Library & Information Technology Association)
Awards & Scholarships
<http://www.lita.org/ala/lita/litaresources/litascholarships/litascholarships.cfm>

Lois Lenski Foundation
Grants for Libraries Serving At-Risk Children
<http://www.cbcbooks.org/pdfs/coveygrantapp.pdf>

Lowes Charitable and Educational Foundation
Toolbox for Education
<http://www.toolboxforeducation.com/>

Outdoor Classroom Grant Program
<http://www.lowes.com/lowes/lkn?action=pg&p=AboutLowes/outdoor/index.html>

National Endowment for the Arts
The Big Read
<http://www.neabigread.org/application_process.php>

NEA Foundation
Student Achievement Grants
<http://www.neafoundation.org/programs/StudentAchievement_Guidelines.htm>

SLJ/Thomson Gale
Giant Step Award
<http://www.schoollibraryjournal.com/info/CA446097.html>

UNESCO
King Hamad Bin Isa Khalifa Prize for the Use of ICTs in Education
<http://portal.unesco.org/education/en/ev.php-
URL_ID=48730&URL_DO=DO_TOPIC&URL_SECTION=201.html>

U.S. Department of Education
Improving Literacy through School Libraries
<http://www.ed.gov/programs/lsl/index.html>

*This list is not intended to be complete. It is just to get you started and to
help you become familiar with some of the awards and contests available. Each was
current at the time of publication.

Index

H

I

J

K

L

M

N

National Education Association (NEA), 22
National Endowment for the Humanities (NEH), 17
Needs assessment, 46
News conferences, 88

O

Objectives, 12, 47, 49, 52-53, 60, 108-109, 111, 113
    measurable, 54
Office of Postsecondary Education, 28, 101

P

Pagination, 66
Partnerships, 34
Parts of the proposal, 43, 50
Patterns of giving, 14
Personnel, 18, 23, 26, 44-45, 48, 50-52,
   55, 73, 107
Plan of action, 48
PowerPoint, x-xi, xiv, 89
Press conferences, 55
Press release, 86-87, 89
Principal, 3-4, 8, 12, 30, 32, 35, 52-53, 56, 59, 73-74, 87, 93
Private foundations, 14, 16, 109
Problem-based learning, 48
Program manager, 95
Program officer, 40, 42, 110
Project description, 48, 113
    fact sheet, 89
    manager, 35, 52, 82, 95
Proofreading, xiv, 71, 76
Proposal letter, 42, 110
Publication Manual of the American Psychological Association, 71
Publicity, 50, 86, 89

Q

Query letter, 20, 24, 110

R

Reader, 25, 28-31, 34, 40-42, 44-46, 51-52, 57, 59-67, 70-72, 101
    responsibilities, 29
Reading teacher, 53, 90
Reasons for rejection, 79-80
Rejection, 77-83
Reports
    final, 54-55
    fiscal, 57
    interim, 54-55, 94
Request for proposal (RFP), 23, 31, 110
Reviewing grants, 26-27
Revise, 11, 31, 35, 40-41, 67, 69-72, 76, 78-79, 82-83
Rewrite, 40-41, 67, 69-70, 79
Rubric, 27, 29-30, 65, 110

S

Salaries, 31, 49-51
Sample grant proposals, 58
Schematics, 57
School Library Journal, 19, 88
Scoring rubric, 27, 29-30, 65
Service learning, 60
Shawnee Mission Education Foundation, 27
Shelving, 9
Signature(s), 35, 38, 56-57, 73-76
Site visit(s), 10, 55, 96
Statement of need, 45-46, 60
Statistical Abstract of the United States, 19
Style, 39, 59, 62, 66, 71
Summative evaluation, 53
Supporting documentation, 57
Sustainability, 53, 56
Synonyms, 61, 71

T

Table of contents, 32, 45, 65-66
Task force reports, 46
Tax-exempt status, 56, 74
Teacher Quality Enhancement Grant Program, 28
Technical Development Corporation, 23
Technology Today, 19
Testimonial, 60, 71, 74
Thoreau, Henry David, 37
Time-and-task, 65
Timeline, 7, 34, 48-49, 51, 55, 64-65, 94, 111, 113
Title, 21, 44-45, 50, 69-70, 72-73, 76
        page, 32, 44-45, 66
Tone, 71
Transition words, 63
Travel, 28, 50, 63, 110

U

U.S. Department of Education, 28, 41, 101, 104, 107-111, 122
Office of Postsecondary Education, 28, 101

V

Voice, 32, 62, 71

W

Workshop(s), 9-10, 18, 22-23, 41, 44, 49, 55, 80